BASIC BUSINESS ROLE PLAYS

David Kerridge

DELTA PUBLISHING

© Copyright DELTA Publishing 1998
© Copyright text David Kerridge 1998
© Copyright illustrations Peter Kent 1998

All rights reserved. No reproduction, copy or transmission of this publication may be made without written permission or in accordance with the provisions of the Copyright, Designs and Patents Act 1988, or under the terms of any licence permitting limited copying issued by the Copyright Licensing Agency, 90 Tottenham Court Road, London W1P 9HE.

Permission to copy

The material in this book is copyright. However, the publisher grants permission for copies of the text to be made as follows:

Private purchasers may make copies for use by their own students; school purchasers may make copies for use within and by the staff and students of the school only. This permission to copy does not extend to additional schools or branches of an institution, who should purchase a separate master copy of the book for their own use.

For copying in other circumstances, prior permission in writing must be obtained from DELTA Publishing, 39 Alexandra Road, Addlestone, Surrey, KT15 2PQ, UK.

First published 1998.

ISBN: (Book) 1 900783 31 2   (Cassette) 1 900783 32 0

Printed in the UK by:
Progressive Printing (UK) Ltd.

Design and page make-up by:
Jordan Publishing Design, Salisbury, Wiltshire.

Cover illustration by:
Indent, Reading.

Illustrations by:
Peter Kent (pp. 1, 9, 16, 23; 32, 39, 46, 53, 60, 64, 67) and
Jordan Publishing Design (pp. 2, 16, 41, 43, 47, 48, 63, 67)

A CIP catalogue record for this book is available from the British Library.

Acknowledgements
To Anne Kilraine for her highly professional editorial assistance and advice.

Contents

	Page
Introduction	iv

Student Section

Unit 1:	*At a Hotel*	1
Unit 2:	*Receiving Foreign Visitors*	9
Unit 3:	*Travel Arrangements*	16
Unit 4:	*In a Restaurant*	23
Unit 5:	*Business or Sport?*	32
Unit 6:	*Slot-machine Food*	39
Unit 7:	*Supermarkets or Shops?*	46
Unit 8:	*Choosing a Supplier*	53
Unit 9:	*Closing a Hospital*	60
Unit 10:	*Fireworks*	67

Teacher Section

Tapescript	76
Teacher's Notes and Answer Keys	81

Unit Language Contents

Unit No	Grammar Notes	Functions and Skills Notes
1	Quantity and Frequency	Telephoning language
2	Prepositions of time	Sequencing
3	Uses of the Present Simple	Explaining problems and suggesting solutions
4	Contractions	Restaurant language
5	Relative pronouns, Interrogatives and a Contraction	Asking questions, making excuses and justifications
6	Prepositions of place	Asking for and giving directions
7	Trends and prepositions with numbers	Asking direct open questions
8	Comparative and superlative adjectives	Agreeing and disagreeing
9	First Conditional	Describing cause and effect
10	Future time	Forecasting

INTRODUCTION

WHAT IS IT?

Basic Business Role Plays provides ten self-contained photocopiable units aimed at lower-intermediate business English learners. Each unit contains various classroom activities which reflect their communicative needs. These activities cover pairwork, information exchanges, mini-presentations as well as role plays. The units can be exploited in any order and each is accompanied by two or more audio-cassette inputs.

WHAT DOES IT CONSIST OF?

Most of the units break down into two parts, the first containing short activities which lead up to – but are distinct from – the second, which consists of more sophisticated activities on the same theme, with full group role plays in Units Five to Ten. Each unit contains:

PART ONE
- Introduction (authentic data about the theme of the unit)
- Linking and Exchanging (vocabulary work)
- Listening Activities (A) (listening and fill-in exercises)
- Short Role Plays (usually pairwork activities)
- Grammar and Functions/Skills Notes (relevant to the theme).

PART TWO
- Storyline (a situation)
- Listening Activities (B) (in preparation for a role play)
- Role Play(s) (with roles provided)
- Afterwards (post-activity writing exercises – two per unit)

The Grammar and Functions/Skills associated with each unit can be used to practise/reinforce recently-taught structures or functions. In this way, ***Basic Business Role Plays*** can be easily integrated into an existing syllabus or course book. Also, many of the Part One activities would be suitable for post-elementary learners.

WHAT IS THE LANGUAGE LEVEL?

The aims of ***Basic Business Role Plays*** are to help all pre-vocational or in-service learners of business English to practise the language they will need in given business and social situations. The print and audio inputs to each unit have been tailored so that the activities and role plays are adapted to the language expertise of lower-intermediate learners.

WHAT ARE THE LEARNERS' NEEDS?

At this level, learners generally have a grasp of basic time patterns (past, present and future) and can ask and answer simple direct questions. However, they probably have difficulty in describing problems, requesting information and expressing agreement or otherwise. The print and audio progression through each unit is designed to help them in these particular skills.

WHAT ARE THE THEMES?

The first four units of ***Basic Business Role Plays*** deal with the situations encountered by most business people (travel problems, receiving foreign visitors etc.). Units Five to Ten move out to themes of common interest (e.g. sport, vending machines and public health). Although these are not traditional 'business themes' at first view, they can all raise business-oriented problems. For example, most football teams need 'investment' in the form of sponsorship. And it is on these 'business' aspects that the units have been based. Although they have been necessarily simplified, each is presented in an adult manner. There is no reason why role plays for a lower-intermediate level should be *qualitatively* different from those at a more advanced level. A final word on themes – where appropriate, social English activities have been included throughout ***Basic Business Role Plays***.

AND ARE THERE ANY LAUGHS?

Yes, perhaps a few. But humour is a risky terrain, usually best avoided by text book writers. But two points should be made here, the first practical, the second pedagogical:

- It is rare for a business transaction to pass off without problems or misunderstandings, and these can be treated with humour.
- A sensitive use of humour can help demystify business, especially among younger learners.

Therefore, the light touches in certain of the audio-conversations and role plays add realism as well as serving a pedagogical purpose.

SOME PRACTICAL SUGGESTIONS

Although there are detailed Teacher Notes to accompany each unit, here are some more general suggestions about the exploitation of ***Basic Business Role Plays***:

- The audio-cassette. This contains a variety of native speaker and non-native speaker accents. Throughout ***Basic Business Role Plays***, the role of the cassette is to provide an input that 'sets the scene' for each situation. Thus, they are usually conflictive, reflecting the problems in the role plays that follow. Each cassette conversation should be played as often as necessary, but three or four plays each time should suffice for most groups. The listening comprehension exercises can be exploited in various ways. Instead of using the fill-ins etc. in the book, you may prefer to play the cassette once, asking learners to note key words/ideas, then build up a picture on the board. Or you could give simple listening tasks before playing the cassette (e.g. 'Is John Swift good at his job?' etc.). In this way, the listening comprehension exercises can be seen simply as a written back-up to previously-answered oral questions. Try to vary the way you exploit the cassette inputs. Most learners appreciate having written exercises, but will soon tire of a standard presentation of them.
- In the Unit Teacher Notes there are suggestions as to which words/explanations might need to be pre-taught. This can be done by explanation or with a dictionary. But you are the best judge of what may be difficult for your learners, so do not hesitate to pre-teach any other words/expressions as you think fit.
- Units One to Four need fewer general Teacher Notes. However, classroom management and monitoring is not always easy with pairwork activities, especially in a large class. There's no magic answer to this, of course. But you could try asking two of your more extrovert learners to do the pairwork role play as a 'demonstration' with the rest of the group giving feedback, then repeating it as a whole group activity.

- In Units Five to Ten, six role cards are provided and in the Teacher Notes it is indicated which roles may be dropped in the case of fewer than six participants.
- Fill-in cards are provided (page 75) on which learners can note the key ideas of their roles. Where necessary, a selection of English and non-English names are noted on the role cards. If no names are necessary, learners should use their own.
- Correction and feedback. During a role play the teacher should intervene only in the case of a breakdown of communication. Otherwise he/she should remain silent. The correction and feedback of a role play can be done in various ways:
  - note the errors and correct them later as a group activity (useful in monolingual classes);
  - note individual errors and give feedback individually;
  - record the role play on audio or video cassette (while making notes of individual errors in case of technical failure during recording).

Finally, I hope you and your learners enjoy using ***Basic Business Role Plays***.

David Kerridge

UNIT 1 — *At a Hotel*

Introduction

Did you know that...?

... one of the world's largest hotel groups is Hilton International. It has 281 hotels in the US and another 91 hotels in 44 other countries.

How often do you stay in hotels? Do you prefer modern or traditional hotels?

Linking and exchanging

1 *Business or holidays?* All hotels have bedrooms, but there are other facilities too:

a night-club	a secretarial service	a bar
fax machines	a restaurant	room service
a crèche	TV	foreign exchange
a swimming pool	a laundry service	conference rooms

Now put these facilities under the correct headings below:

Business hotels	Holiday hotels	Both

2 Where do the following hotel personnel work? Draw lines to link them:

The manager	in the kitchen
The bar staff	in an office
The chef	behind the bar
The waiters and waitresses	at the reception desk
The receptionist	in the restaurant

3 Who does what? Draw lines to link the following verbs and nouns:

HOTEL PERSONNEL		
The receptionist	pour	the hotel.
The manager	serve	drinks.
The bar staff	prepares	guests.
The waiters and waitresses	welcomes	at tables.
The chef	manages	the menus.

4 In most hotel bedrooms you will find the following things. Link the word to the drawing and write the answer in the space provided.

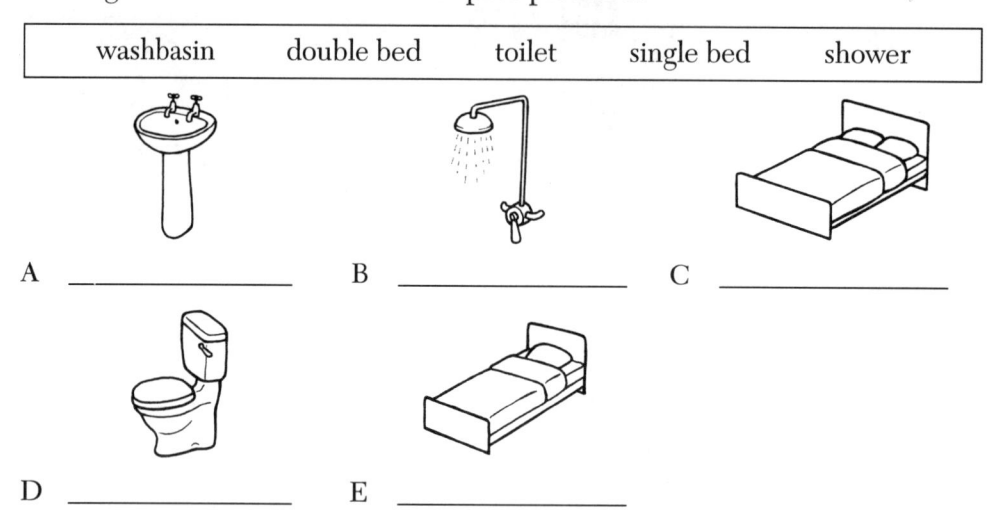

| washbasin | double bed | toilet | single bed | shower |

A _____   B _____   C _____

D _____   E _____

In hotel bedrooms you can also find:
- a clothes cupboard;
- towels;
- soap;
- a mini-bar;
- coat hangers;
- a writing table.

And most hotels have a morning call system.

GRAMMAR NOTES: QUANTITY AND FREQUENCY

Quantity

Match the approximate quantity words with their percentage equivalents. Write the correct word in the space provided.

Exact		**Approximate**
100%	_____	some
85%	_____	none/no
70%	_____	all
40%	_____	little/few
20%	_____	many/much
0%	_____	most

Frequency

Put these frequency adverbs in <u>descending</u> order. The first one has been done for you.

| often | always | never | usually | sometimes |

1 __always__　　　　　　　　4 _____

2 _____　　　　　　　　5 _____

3 _____

SKILLS NOTES: TELEPHONING

Introducing yourself – 'Good morning. My name's…'
　　　　　　　　　　　 'Good afternoon. This is…'
Saying what you want – 'I'd like to…'
　　　　　　　　　　　 'Can I…?'
Asking for information – 'Can you tell me if…?'
　　　　　　　　　　　 'Do you have a …?'
　　　　　　　　　　　 'Is there a…?'

5 Now listen to a telephone conversation between a client and a hotel receptionist, and fill in the blanks in the details below:

The hotel receptionist noted:

```
ACCOMMODATION RESERVATION FORM

Family name_____    First name _____
Arrival date_____    Departure date _____
Accommodation_____     Room number ____13_____
Payment_____   Confirmation_____
```

The client noted:

> Name of hotel　　Schiller
> TV　　　　　　　OK
> Price of room
> Price of breakfast
> Fax number

6 *Polite requests: affirmative and negative replies.*

Now listen to the conversation again and fill in the missing words.

1　Good afternoon, _____ _____ _____ book a room, please.

2　_____, madam. When for, please?

3　_____ _____ we only have showers.

4　_____ you give me your name, please?

5　_____ you confirm this by fax, please?

Role plays – Making reservations

ROLE PLAY ONE — A

You are the receptionist of the Excelsior Hotel in Buenos Aires (Argentina). Here are some details about the hotel:
- All rooms with showers and toilets.
- All rooms with colour TV (but not cable or satellite).
- Bar, but no restaurant.
- Private car park.

Room prices: 50 dollars/night
Breakfast: 5 dollars
Car parking space: 4 dollars/night

Note: Rooms are available for the dates requested.

ROLE PLAY ONE — B

Your name is Johanna/Johan Fitzbender. Telephone the Excelsior Hotel in Buenos Aires (Argentina). You want to book:
- a single room with shower and toilet;
- for 13–17 April (four nights);
- a car parking space.

You want to know:
- the price of the rooms;
- the prices of breakfast and the parking space;
- if your room has satellite TV;
- if the hotel has a restaurant.

ROLE PLAY TWO — A

You are the receptionist of the King Charles Hotel in Prague (the Czech Republic). Here are some details about the hotel:
- Most of the rooms with toilets and baths, some with showers.
- All rooms with colour TV.
- Bar and restaurant.
- No private car park (but public car park nearby).

Room prices (including breakfast): 1600 crowns/night (without bath)
                                   220 crowns/night (with bath or shower)

Dinner: 600 crowns (standard menu)
        750 crowns (special menu)

Note: Rooms are available for the dates requested.

ROLE PLAY TWO — B

Your name is Mary/Michael Tyndall. Telephone the King Charles Hotel in Prague (the Czech Republic). You will travel to Prague with two colleagues. You want to reserve:
- three single rooms with bath;
- for 4–6 September (two nights);
- a car parking space.

You want to know:
- the price of the rooms;
- if the hotel has a restaurant;
- the price of dinner (one of your colleagues is a vegetarian);
- if the rooms have TV.

1 At a Hotel © delta Publishing 1998

Storyline

Read the text below.

The London-based Hayes Hotel Group has business hotels in many countries in Europe. Each hotel has single and double rooms, suites, a restaurant, conference rooms and a secretarial service.

John Swift is the English manager of the Hayes Hotel in Hamburg (Germany). But he is not very efficient and this has caused problems.

1 Now listen to the cassette and then do the exercises.
Are the following statements true (T) or false (F)? Circle the correct answers.

   1 The client booked a room by telephone.   T   F
   2 She did not confirm by fax.   T   F
   3 She accepts the suite.   T   F
   4 She goes to another hotel.   T   F
   5 She is not satisfied.   T   F

2 Complete the following details:

   Client's family name: _____

   Price of suite: _____

   Name of alternative hotel: _____

3 *1* Someone made a mistake about the client's reservation. What was the mistake? _____

   2 Why did the client refuse John Swift's suggestion?
   _____

   3 What did the client do?
   _____

Role plays – Complaints and requests

ROLE PLAY THREE A

You have just arrived in your room at the Hayes Hotel in Hamburg. It is 10.30 in the evening. You have two problems:
- no coat hangers in your clothes cupboard;
- mini-bar empty (you are thirsty).

Go down to the reception desk and speak to the night receptionist.

ROLE PLAY THREE B

You are the night receptionist at the Hayes Hotel in Hamburg. It is 10.30 in the evening. Ten minutes ago a guest arrived and went to his/her room. He/she will return to the reception desk to explain two problems.

Notes:
- hotel bar closed (only John Swift has keys);
- coat hangers in John Swift's office, but door locked;
- John Swift has gone home (lives 15 kilometres away).

How can you help the guest? Use your imagination.

ROLE PLAY FOUR A1

You are Magda/Marius Kalovitch. You are staying at the Hayes Hotel in Hamburg. Telephone reception and ask for a morning call for tomorrow at 7.00. Your room number is 17.

(There are no towels in your room.)

ROLE PLAY FOUR A2

It is 9.15 the next morning. You did not receive a morning call, and are late for an important meeting at K A Metall.

Go to reception. You want:
- a taxi immediately;
- the Hayes Hotel to pay for the taxi;
- the receptionist to telephone K A Metall to explain why you will be late.

You are very dissatisfied!

ROLE PLAY FOUR B1

You are the receptionist at the Hayes Hotel in Hamburg.
You will receive a telephone call from one of your guests. Get his/her name and room number and note his/her request(s).

ROLE PLAY FOUR B2

It is 9.15 the next morning. Something has gone wrong and your guest is not satisfied. Try to help him/her.

Note: You do not think the Hayes Hotel will pay for a taxi.

ROLE PLAY FIVE A

You are Michelle/Michel Lebras. You are staying at the Hayes Hotel in Hamburg. Yesterday you asked the hotel secretary to write and send a fax confirming a meeting with a colleague in Madrid. John Swift has just given you a copy of the fax. Here it is:

```
                    FAX
    Manuel Ortez
    Electricon
    Madrid

    Dear Ortez
    The meeting is good for 25
    june. I arriving at 24 july
    at 22 o'clock.
    Affectionately
            Michel/Michelle
```

How many mistakes can you find?
Now go back to John Swift and complain. Then together write a second fax with corrected dates and text.
Note: The cost of writing and sending a fax is DM 50 per page. You do not want to pay for these faxes because of the secretary's mistakes.

ROLE PLAY FIVE B

You are John Swift, manager of the Hayes Hotel in Hamburg. One of your guests, Michelle/Michel Lebras, has a problem with a fax. Try to help him/her.
Notes:
- usual hotel secretary on holiday;
- temporary secretary not very efficient;
- cost of writing and sending a fax: DM 50 per page.

DISCUSSION

You are the Directors of the Hayes Hotel Group at its London headquarters. Recently you have received several complaints about your hotel in Hamburg. First, go back through the unit and list the weak points of John Swift's management. Then discuss how things can be improved.

Note: You cannot dismiss John Swift. He is the son of your Managing Director.

Afterwards

1 Here is the fax which the Directors of the Hayes Hotel Group sent to John Swift. Read it, choosing the correct word in italics in the first two paragraphs. The third paragraph will be the recommendations of your group following your meeting.

FAX

Dear John,

At a recent *Directors'/Director's* meeting, we noticed that there have been a *numerous/number* of complaints about the Hayes Hotel in Hamburg. We are very *concerning/concerned* about this, because complaints can *affect/effect* our reputation badly.

Therefore, we suggest that you *make/take* the following steps to improve the way you manage the hotel:

1 _____
2 _____
3 _____

Please act on this fax urgently and report back in two weeks.

Regards

---

2 Put the information in the box into the correct place in the hotel reservation form below:

| Blackwell | approx. 6 p.m. | £65/night | 7 April | 0131 869 9583 |
| 9 April | 215 | George | credit card | single + shower |

BURNS HOTEL – EDINBURGH

Family name _____	Arrival date _____
First name _____	Departure date _____
Telephone _____	Arrival time _____
Type of room _____	Price £ _____
Room number _____	Payment _____

UNIT 2 Receiving Foreign Visitors

Introduction

Did you know that…?

> …business travellers spend US$450 billion per year on their trips.
> …in 1996, only 13% of the passengers at London's Heathrow Airport were British.

How often does your company receive foreign visitors? What are their nationalities? Why do they come?

Linking and exchanging

1 *Saying hello: the right expression.* Link the correct greeting with the circumstances.

A mixed group	(8.00 a.m.)	'Good afternoon, ladies.'
A group of women	(3.00 p.m.)	'Good morning, ladies and gentlemen.'
A group of men	(9.00 a.m.)	'Morning, everybody.'
Colleagues	(10.00 a.m.)	'Hello, everybody.'
Colleagues	(any time)	'Good morning, gentlemen.'

Notes:
- We do not *say* 'Greetings'.
- 'Goodnight' means 'Goodbye' (in the evening).
- 'Hi' is very informal.
- Obviously, we use other expressions, but the above are best in formal circumstances.

10

Welcoming visitors: ordering and sequencing.

In the reception area of Bailey Instruments plc, Jennie Knight, the Public Relations Officer is welcoming a group of visitors.

2 Listen to the cassette and put the five events she mentions *into the order they will happen*.

A R & D department	1
B Jennie Knight's presentation	2
C lunch	3
D coffee	4
E Production department	5

3 Now listen again and fill in the words/phrases Jennie used.

1 _____, we'll go into the meeting room…

2 _____, my colleague, Jeremy Stevens…

3 … the Production department _____ Myriam Snowden…

4 …the R & D department. _____ we'll have lunch…

5 But _____, let's have coffee.

4 ***Offering, and making small talk***. Read this short conversation between Jennie Knight (JK) and one of the visitors (V). Then put in the correct question forms from the box beside the text.

JK: _____ a coffee?

V: Yes, please.

JK: Sugar?

V: No, thank you.

JK: _____ a good trip?

V: Not really. My plane was delayed.

JK: _____ happened?

V: Fog at the airport, but the flight was OK.

JK: _____ like?

V: Fine, very comfortable.

JK: _____ Bailey easily?

V: Oh, yes. Your instructions were very clear.

JK: I think it's time for the presentation now, so let's…

```
What's your hotel
Would you like
Oh? What
And did you find
Did you have
```

Now you will receive a group of visitors from another country. Using your own name and company:

- say hello;
- introduce yourself;
- offer coffee;
- ask about your visitors' trips/hotels etc.…

5 *Talking about companies*. In her presentation to the visitors, Jennie Knight probably used some of the following verbs and noun phrases. Link them up in the grid on the right.

Bailey Instruments:

a	was founded	1	microscopes.
b	moved	2	on an industrial estate.
c	exports	3	finished goods in a warehouse.
d	manufactures	4	a turnover of £20m.
e	has	5	to Europe and South America.
f	expanded	6	from London to Swansea in 1992.
g	is situated	7	a profit last year of £1.7m.
h	employs	8	in 1984.
i	made	9	its production facilities by 30%.
j	stocks	10	150 people.

a	
b	
c	
d	
e	
f	
g	
h	
i	
j	

GRAMMAR NOTES

Prepositions of time

on, *in* or *at*? Put in the correct preposition.

1 She founded the company ____ 1994.
2 'I'll see you ____ Wednesday ____ 11 o'clock.
3 Production fell ____ May.
4 'Let's meet ____ the end of the month, ____ the 29th, if that's OK.'
5 Sales always fall ____ the winter.

SKILLS NOTES: SEQUENCING

When Jennie Knight spoke to her visitors, she used the following words to describe sequences:

in a few minutes, following that, then, after that, first

Other sequencing words are:

to begin with, secondly, later, afterwards, finally

You will need to use some of these words later on in the unit.

Storyline

1 Link the following words by drawing lines.

waterproof	professional sailors
seamen	holiday sailing
local outlets	water-resistant
leisure sailing	local markets

2 *Facts and figures.* Listen to the cassette and fill in the gaps.

1 Paco Cordobes is the _____ Manager of Vestimenta del Mar.
2 Vestimenta del Mar manufactures clothing for _____.
3 The company was founded in _____.
4 Spain joined the European Union in _____.
5 The regional warehouses are in _____ and _____.
6 Vestimenta del Mar exports _____ of its production.
7 The company employs about _____ people.
8 There are _____ production staff and _____ sales people.
9 Clothing for seamen represents _____ % of domestic sales.
10 Light waterproof clothing represents _____ % of sales.

3 *Language of presentations.* Now listen again and fill in the blanks.

1 (Introducing subject) 'First _____ the company,'
2 (Introducing subject) 'then, _____ future developments.'
3 (Referring to visual) 'As _____ slide, our activities…'
4 (Changing subject) 'Right, _____ personnel.'
5 (Changing subject) 'Now _____ our products and sales.'

4 *Comprehension.* Choose the best answers to the following.

1 During the 60s and 70s, the company (a) sold products in Vigo.
   (b) exported to the EU.
2 Vestimenta del Mar has (a) warehouses in different parts of Spain.
   (b) warehouses only in Vigo.
3 Most of the employees work (a) in Barcelona.
   (b) in Vigo.
4 The leisure sailing market is (a) based in France.
   (b) getting bigger.

Role plays

Here are some general notes for presenters and visitors.

Presenter

You will present your company to a group of foreign visitors.

Your teacher will give you details.

Remember the following stages:
- words of welcome;
- introduction of yourself and your job;
- details of coffee, toilets etc.;
- social English to the group.

Then make your presentation as follows:
- products or services;
- history of company;
- head office and other offices;
- number and categories of employees;
- present markets.

And finish your presentation by asking for questions. You can say:
- 'Are there any questions?'
- 'Does anybody have questions?'

Visitors

You will be in a group of visitors to a company. Perhaps you can ask:
- where the toilets are;
- if you can make a telephone call;
- where you can put your coat;
- if you can have orange juice instead of coffee.

During the presentation, *ask* if there is something you do not understand. You can say:
- 'Can you repeat/clarify that, please?'
- 'Can you speak more slowly, please?'
- 'Excuse me, what does X mean, please?'

COMPANY A

Presenter

Your name:	Juanita/Juan Cardenas
Your job:	Managing Director
Company:	Turismo y Civilisacion, founded 1989
Product/service:	tourism
Head office:	Mexico City
Employees:	3 managers and 6 guides
Company activities:	tours to Aztec and Mayan sites
Accommodation:	local hotels
Travel:	air or coach
Guides:	experienced, trilingual (Spanish, English, French)

Notes:
- Your visitors – travel agents from different countries.
- Tourism to Mexico going up.
- Most tourists from Europe or US.
- More than 3,000 clients last year.

COMPANY A

Visitors

You are visitors to: Turismo y Civilisacion, in Mexico.
You are travel agents from different countries.
You want to know about the possibilities for tourism to Aztec and Mayan sites in Mexico.

COMPANY B

Presenter

Your name:	Janeta/Janos Varga
Your job:	Production Manager
Company:	Magyar Materials, founded 1970
Product/service:	fibreglass
Head office and factory:	30 km south of Budapest
Employees:	45 production staff
	15 administrative and sales staff
	6 managers
Company activities:	Originally a plastics factory, modernised in 1992. Manufactures bodies for cars and pleasure boats.
Markets:	internal – 65%
	export (European Union) – 12%
	export (Central Europe) – 23%
Future:	hope to expand exports to European Union.

Notes:
- Your visitors – business people from Poland.
- Hungary will join the European Union in the near future.

COMPANY B

Visitors

You are visitors to: Magyar Materials, near Budapest in Hungary.
You are business people from Poland.
You want to look at the company's modernised production facilities.

COMPANY C

Presenter

Your name:	Maria/Mario da Silva
Your job:	Director
Company:	Vinos da Costa Verde
Product/service:	port wines
Office (and vineyards):	30 km north of Porto
Employees:	23 permanent staff
	8 administrative staff
	(plus about 50 seasonal workers)
Company activities:	Founded in 18th century (exact date not known) – small producer, with long history of export to UK. Your family bought company in 1912.
Markets:	internal – 28%
	UK – 19%
	European Union – 21%
	other countries – 32%
Future:	uncertain, hope to export to Central Europe and Asia

Notes:
- Your visitors – US and UK wine importers.
- Portugal joined the European Union in 1986.

COMPANY C

Visitors

You are visitors to: Vinos da Costa Verde, near Porto in Portugal.
You are British and American wine importers.
You want to hear about the company, and you hope to taste the wine after the presentation.

Afterwards

1 *Writing*. In your three 'visitors' groups write a letter of thanks, filling in the gaps with your own ideas.

Date _____

Dear _____

We are writing to thank _____
_____
_____
_____

We were particularly interested in _____
_____
_____

because _____
_____
_____

We look forward to _____
_____
_____

Once again, our thanks for your hospitality.

Yours _____

---

2 Link these verbs to their opposites by drawing lines.

export	gain
expand	import
lose	stop
fall	contract
start	rise

Now put some of these verbs into the sentences below, using the right tense.

1 They will _____ in efficiency by using computers.
2 1997 was a good year. Profits _____.
3 The company _____ computers from Taiwan.
4 We _____ our marketing into South America last year.
5 Two years ago they _____ selling cigarettes in Europe because of falling profits.

UNIT 3 *Travel Arrangements*

Introduction

Did you know that...?

- ... the four airports of New York have the largest number of flights in the world – about 10,000 domestic and 2,000 overseas flights per week.
- ... Virgin Atlantic give in-flight massage in Business Class, that Lufthansa give tapes with English lessons and that Iberia has a *very* large wine selection!

Do you travel for your job? Where do you go? What problems do you have? How do you travel? How long for?

Linking and exchanging

1 Most business travellers use airports, but do you know the 'language of airports'? Look at the signs then write the correct word from the box in the space provided.

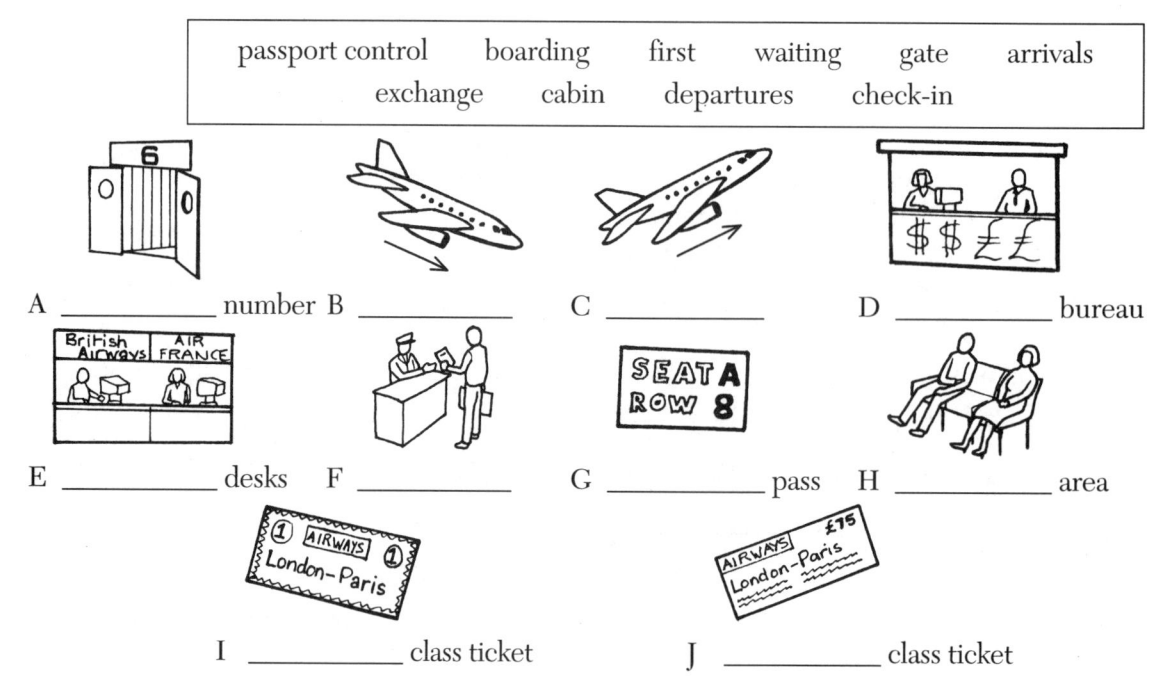

| passport control | boarding | first | waiting | gate | arrivals |
| exchange | cabin | departures | check-in |

A _____ number   B _____   C _____   D _____ bureau

E _____ desks   F _____   G _____ pass   H _____ area

I _____ class ticket   J _____ class ticket

3 Travel Arrangements   © Delta Publishing 1998
· This page may be photocopied under the terms outlined on p.ii.

2 *Travel problems: causes and consequences*. Link the following by drawing lines to make logical sentences.

The flight was delayed	but she overslept.
The Hayes hotel was fully booked	so they went by Eurostar.
Flights to Brussels were cancelled	so he was late for the meeting.
The train left on time	but the meeting was at 4.00 p.m.
She arrived at 9.00 a.m.	so they stayed in another one.

Have you experienced these problems?

3 Read the following text then link the words in italics to their definitions in the box below.

Dr. Andrea Matthews is the *Research* Director of Jameson Laboratories, *based* in Bedford in the UK. She often *attends* international congresses and makes about fifteen business *trips* per year. Angela Davies is her Personal Assistant. She *arranges* the necessary plane and hotel *bookings*.

research	situated
based	organises
attends	reservations
trips	investigation
arranges	journeys
bookings	goes to

4 *Comprehension*. Andrea Matthews is at the Lufthansa check-in desk at Heathrow Airport (London). Listen to the cassette, then answer the questions below.

1 The *beginning* of the conversation: What does Andrea Matthews want to know?

_____

2 The *middle* of the conversation: What has happened to the flight?

_____

3 The *middle* of the conversation: What are the consequences for Andrea Matthews?

_____

4 The *end* of the conversation: What does the Lufthansa check-in clerk offer to do?

_____

5 *Offers and requests: problems and consequences*. Listen again and fill in the gaps below.

1 _____ _____ _____ _____, madam?
2 _____ _____ _____ _____ ticket, please?
3 _____ _____ but take-off has…
4 About an hour, _____ _____.
5 _____ _____ I'll be late for…
6 _____ _____ _____ a seat?

Role plays

ROLE PLAY ONE   A

You arrive at Heathrow Airport (London). You are booked on a flight to Madrid which leaves in one hour. You have your ticket, but have forgotten your passport. Explain the situation to your partner, an airline check-in clerk.

ROLE PLAY ONE   B

You are a check-in clerk at Heathrow Airport (London). Suggest that your partner goes to see the Customs Officers. Perhaps they will give him/her a temporary travel document.

ROLE PLAY TWO   A

You arrive late at the airport, have missed your flight to Hamburg and will be late for a meeting. Ask the information desk clerk about other flights. Then ask if you can make a telephone call to Germany.

ROLE PLAY TWO   B

You work at an airport information desk. Your partner will explain his/her problem. The next flight to his/her destination is in two hours. Seats are available. There are public telephone boxes in the waiting area.

ROLE PLAY THREE   A

You are at a railway station. You want to book a second-class seat on a train from Paris to Vienna for tomorrow at 10 a.m.

ROLE PLAY THREE   B

You are a travel agent. There are no more second-class seats on the 10 a.m. train from Paris to Vienna tomorrow. There are first-class seats, or second-class couchettes on the train tomorrow night.

GRAMMAR NOTES: USES OF THE PRESENT SIMPLE

We use the present simple to describe facts or actions that usually or regularly take place, or are 'permanent' events. For example:

She works in Manchester.   *He always travels first class.*   *Athens is hot in the summer.*

We also use the present simple when talking about timetables. For example:

'Your flight leaves at 09:00 tomorrow.'   *'That train never arrives on time.'*

FUNCTIONS/SKILLS NOTES: EXPLAINING PROBLEMS AND SUGGESTING SOLUTIONS

Explaining problems
I'm afraid there's a problem…
You see,…

Suggesting solutions
Yes, I understand/I see…
Why don't you…?
You should…
Can't you…

Some of these expressions will be useful in the role plays that follow.

Storyline

Here is the travel programme that Angela Davies arranged for Andrea Matthews:

```
              JAMESON LABORATORIES
   Travel programme - trip to Germany and Poland
                Dr Andrea Matthews

   Destination      Dates       Flight No:   Depart   Arrive
   London-Berlin    5 April     LH 4501      10:30    12:40
   Berlin-Warsaw    7 April     LH 2540      09:00    10:00
   Warsaw-London    10 April    BA 851       15:30    17:50

   Hotels
   Berlin: Linden Hotel      5-7 April  (2 nights)
   Warsaw: Old Market Hotel  7-10 April (3 nights)
```

1 It is the afternoon of 6 April. Angela Davies receives a telephone call from Andrea Matthews. Listen to their conversation and decide if the following statements are true (T) or false (F):

1. Andrea Matthews wants to cancel her visit to Warsaw.   T F
2. She has an appointment in Warsaw on 8 April.   T F
3. She wants to change the appointment.   T F
4. She tried to telephone someone in Warsaw.   T F
5. Angela will telephone Andrea the next morning.   T F
6. She asks Angela to buy a bottle of vodka.   T F
7. Problems are frequent during Andrea's business trips.   T F

2
1. Why does Andrea ask Angela to change her appointment?

   _____

2. What is the date and time of the original appointment?

   _____

3. What new date and time does Andrea ask for?

   _____

4. Did Andrea telephone Dr Kalowska? What was the result?

   _____

5. What does Angela promise to do? _____

6. What is 'her price'? _____

3 Listen to the cassette again and fill in the gaps below:

1. *A problem.* '…till the 8th. _____ _____ _____ _____ , I've …'

2. *A request.* 'So _____ _____ _____ _____ tomorrow morning and…'

3. *A suggestion.* 'But why _____ _____ –'

4. *Intention.* 'OK, Andrea. _____ _____ it and send you…'

3 Travel Arrangements   © Delta Publishing 1998

Role plays – Telephoning and faxing

Work in groups of three. In the following role plays, you will try to solve different travel problems. You will make at least two telephone calls and write a short fax. All the role plays are about the following situation, so read this carefully:

Aardvark Furniture is a multinational Danish company based in Copenhagen (Denmark). It is planning to have a conference for its European Sales Managers. The conference will be at the Rif Conference Centre near Casablanca (in Morocco) on 11–14 October.

In Morocco, the conference organiser is Salma/Samir Bekkali, who works at the Rif Conference Centre.

In Denmark, the person responsible for all enquiries is Sonja/Sven Alborg, who works at the head office of Aardvark in Copenhagen.

ROLE PLAY FOUR — A1

Your name: Janet/John Marshall
Your job: Sales Manager, Aardvark Furniture (UK)
Your problem: You want to bring your partner (Florence/Florent Duvilliers) to the conference.
You want to:
- book an extra air ticket, and
- reserve a double room.

(Your partner will pay for his/her expenses.)

Telephone Sonja/Sven Alborg

ROLE PLAY FOUR — A2

Telephone Sonja/Sven Alborg with your reply

ROLE PLAY FOUR — B1

You are: Sonja/Sven Alborg
Someone will telephone you.
Note what he/she wants.
Say you will reply by fax.

ROLE PLAY FOUR — B2

Telephone Salma/Samir Bekkali. Ask for the necessary changes to Janet/John Marshall's booking.
Agree with Salma's/Samir's suggestion.

ROLE PLAY FOUR — B3

Send a fax to Janet/John Marshall.

ROLE PLAY FOUR — B4

Send a fax to Salma/Samir Bekkali.

ROLE PLAY FOUR C

You are: Salma/Samir Bekkali
Someone will telephone you.
The call will be about Janet/John Marshall – a participant at the Aardvark conference.
Note all necessary details.
Situation:
- no double rooms at conference centre;
- possible in nearby Majestic Hotel;
- Majestic Hotel expensive: 740 dirhams/night for a double room.

Suggest: a provisional reservation (to be confirmed by fax).

ROLE PLAY FIVE A

Your name: Ulrike/Ulrich Brandt
Your job: Sales Manager, Aardvark Furniture (Germany)
Your problem: After the conference, you want to tour the Moroccan Sahara (one week).
You want:
- to hire a jeep and a tent;
- road maps of Morocco.

Telephone Sonja/Sven Alborg.

ROLE PLAY FIVE B1

You are: Sonja/Sven Alborg
Someone will telephone you.
Make a note of what he/she wants.
Say you will reply by fax.

ROLE PLAY FIVE B2

Someone will telephone you.
Note down all details and suggestions.

ROLE PLAY FIVE B3

Send a fax to Ulrike/Ulrich Brandt.

ROLE PLAY FIVE C1

You are: Salma/Samir Bekkali
Someone will telephone you.
Note all the details (including dates).
Situation:
- the Rif Conference Centre cannot help directly;
- you will contact a travel agent in Casablanca and ring your caller back.

ROLE PLAY FIVE C2

Here are the details the travel agent gave you:
- hire of jeeps expensive;
- no tents for hire.

Telephone Sonja/Sven Alborg.
Suggest organised tour in Land Rover with hotel accommodation (5750 dirhams for 8 days).

ROLE PLAY SIX — A1

Your name: Maria/Mario Salvini
Your job: Sales Manager, Aardvark Furniture (Italy)
Your problem: You will give a presentation on 13 October.
You want to check that you will have a microphone.
Also, you want someone to record your presentation on video.
Telephone Sonja/Sven Alborg.

ROLE PLAY SIX — A2

Decide on your reaction then telephone Sonja/Sven Alborg.

ROLE PLAY SIX — B1

You are: Sonja/Sven Alborg
Someone will telephone you.
Make a note about what he/she wants.
Say you will reply by fax.

ROLE PLAY SIX — B2

Telephone Salma/Samir Bekkali and ask about Salvini's requests.
Note down information and send fax to Maria/Mario Salvini.

ROLE PLAY SIX — C

You are: Salma/Samir Bekkali
Someone will telephone you.
Note down his/her requests and information.
Situation:
- microphone OK;
- cost of video recording (camera and operator): 4125 dirhams/day

Suggest: audio recording (free).

Afterwards

Read this conversation between David Bridges (DB) and a colleague (C) and circle the correct word from the three given (in italics):

C: Well, what was the conference like?

DB: Terrible! Everything went (1) *left/right/wrong*. First, I (2) *overslept/slept over/under-slept* and (3) *missed/reserved/caught* my train, and then the taxi to the hotel (4) *broke in/broke up/broke down*, and when I arrived at the hotel, they told me there was no (5) *cancellation/booking/waiting list* in my name. They (6) *arranged/appointed/approached* a room in another hotel, but it was 5 km from the conference centre.

C: So you could (7) *assist at/wait/attend* the conference?

DB: Oh, yes. But it was (8) *badly-enterprised/staged/organised*. None of the presentations began (9) *on time/by time/at time* and the microphones didn't work so I (10) *can't/couldn't/shouldn't* hear anything. So I left after the first day.

UNIT 4 — *In a Restaurant*

Introduction

Did you know that...?

- ... in the US, the restaurant industry employs over 9 million people. The number of fast food restaurants in America stood at 32,000 in 1970, rose to 86,000 by 1987 and is now much higher.

Do you eat in fast food restaurants?
What are their advantages?

Linking and exchanging

1 *Restaurant pleasures*. Link the phrases below with the pictures. Write the letter in the box beside the correct phrase.

A B C D E

1 'Johnny, use your fork.'
2 'This glass is dirty!'
3 'I've forgotten my wallet.'
4 'Not much room, is there?'
5 'They said it was a non-smoking restaurant.'

4 In a Restaurant   © Delta Publishing 1998
This page may be photocopied under the terms outlined on p.ii.

2 *In a restaurant*. Link the phrases below with their responses. Write the correct number in the box.

a I'd like to reserve a table for Saturday.
b Which wine do you recommend?
c This knife's dirty!
d Another bottle of the same, please.
e Is service included?
f Are you ready to order?
g Do you accept cheques?
h How would you like your steak, sir?

1 The Beaujolais Villages is very good.
2 Yes, it is, sir.
3 For how many people, please?
4 I'll change it immediately.
5 Medium, please.
6 Certainly. Or a credit card if you prefer.
7 No, not yet.
8 Certainly, madam. I'll bring it now.

a	
b	
c	
d	
e	
f	
g	
h	

3 Garry Jones and his partner, Sammy Watkins decided to open a restaurant in their town. Two weeks before opening, they wrote out a menu and showed it to their chef, who first made some spelling corrections and then improved the choice in the menu.

Here is the original menu. What spelling mistakes did the chef correct?

```
Oasis Restaurant

Starters        Veggetable soup
                Tomatoe salade

Main coarses    Fish and chips
                Griled steaks

Deserts         Aple pie

                Cofee
```

Note: there are eight spelling mistakes on the original menu.

4 The Oasis Restaurant opened on a Saturday evening, but it was not a success. Now listen to the cassette and answer the questions below.

Conversation one
Fill in the missing information.

The customer, Mrs Hoskins, (1) _____ a table for (2) _____

people. When the manager took her to the table, she was not satisfied because

(3) _____.

Conversation two

Answer questions 1 and 2 then fill in the missing words (3–7).

1 Why is the customer dissatisfied? _____
2 What does the waiter reply? _____
3 '_____ you _____ _____ _____, sir?'
4 'Ready? We've _____ _____ for _____ _____ _____.'
5 '_____ _____, sir. But _____ _____ _____, you see.'
6 'Why _____ _____ get _____ _____?'
7 'Well, we've _____ _____ _____ and…'

Conversation three

Circle TRUE, FALSE or DON'T KNOW beside the following statements (1–4), then fill in the waitress's words (5 and 6).

1 The Oasis Restaurant accepts cheques.   TRUE/FALSE/DON'T KNOW
2 The Oasis Restaurant accepts credit cards.   TRUE/FALSE/DON'T KNOW
3 Charlie has lost his cheque book.   TRUE/FALSE/DON'T KNOW
4 Charlie's companion pays.   TRUE/FALSE/DON'T KNOW

The waitress says:

5 'Here's _____ _____ , sir.'
6 'I'm _____ _____ _____ _____ _____ , sir.'

Role plays – Restaurant problems

ROLE PLAY ONE	A

You have invited an important client to lunch at the Oasis Restaurant. The person at the next table is making and receiving a lot of calls on his/her mobile phone. He/she has a loud voice and laughs a lot. Politely ask him/her to turn off the mobile phone. If he/she doesn't stop, call the waiter/waitress.

ROLE PLAY ONE	B

You are having lunch at the Oasis Restaurant. You are making and receiving a lot of business calls on your mobile phone. Insist on continuing. The calls are urgent.

ROLE PLAY ONE	C

You are a waiter/waitress at the Oasis Restaurant. One of the customers will call you. Try to help him/her. Use your imagination.

ROLE PLAY TWO — A

You are a customer at the Oasis Restaurant. You have just received your bill:

You do not want to pay for your dessert (the fruit salad was not fresh, but you ate it) and you drank only a glass of wine (£1.20) not a carafe. Call the waiter/waitress.

	£ p
Main course	15.20
Dessert	3.75
Carafe of wine	4.75
Coffee	1.15

ROLE PLAY TWO — B

You are a waiter/waitress at the Oasis Restaurant. You have just given a bill to a customer. He/she will call you back.

Notes:
- he/she drank one glass of wine;
- he/she didn't complain about the dessert.

ROLE PLAY THREE — A

Your name: Nathalie/Nick Archer

You have reserved a corner table for dinner in the Oasis Restaurant at 8.00 p.m. You want to be isolated because you will have a confidential business discussion with your guest. You arrive at the restaurant. Give your name to the manager.

ROLE PLAY THREE — B

You are the manager of the Oasis Restaurant. It is 8.00 p.m. You will receive two customers. Ask for the name, then try to help them.

Notes:
- all corner tables full;
- possible to share a table in centre of room;
- possibility of private room (£35 extra);
- private room not free till 9.00 p.m.

After five months, the Oasis Restaurant closed. This was because of inefficient service and bad organisation. So Garry and Sammy went to work for the American company, Pizza World, whose European headquarters are in London

GRAMMAR NOTES: CONTRACTIONS

Do you remember these remarks from the conversations at the Oasis Restaurant?

'I've reserved a table for three.'
'But it's right beside the toilets.'
'We've been waiting for half an hour.'
'...we don't accept cheques.'
'I'll pay by credit card.'

Note the contracted form when we speak:

Contracted form	Full form
I've reserved	I have reserved
But it's	But it is
We've been waiting	We have been waiting
...we don't accept	...we do not accept
I'll pay	I will pay

Write in the full form beside the contracted form of the following verbs.

1. I've known Pedro for a long time.   I _____
2. He'll be late for the meeting.   He _____
3. She doesn't want that job.   She _____
4. They've been living in Argentina.   They _____
5. He's been writing the report.   He _____
6. I'm going to Milan tomorrow.   I _____
7. She's often visited New York.   She _____
8. They won't renew the contract.   They _____
9. You haven't been to Ghana, have you?   You _____
10. I'll ask her to reserve the hotel rooms.   I _____

FUNCTIONS/SKILLS NOTES: RESTAURANT LANGUAGE

Put the following phrases into the correct order.

1. table for book I'd a like please to four
   _____
2. included service 10% a charge is
   _____
3. like madam to you order would?
   _____
4. cards you take do credit?
   _____
5. order change to want I my
   _____
6. section please smoking the
   _____
7. water have some I please could mineral?
   _____
8. like what starters you would for?
   _____

Storyline

Pizza World is a high-quality Italian-American restaurant company. It was founded by Carlo Ganzetti in New York in 1961. Now it has restaurants in all the major western European cities. Last year it opened two restaurants in Poland (in Warsaw and Cracow) but results have not been good.

The European Director of Pizza World (Jerry Stacks) has come to Warsaw to investigate. Listen to his conversation with Anna Waleska, Director of Pizza World in Poland.

1 Are the following statements true (T) or false (F)?

1. Pizza World has a lot of competitors in Poland.   T   F
2. The Poles think Pizza World is a fast food company.   T   F
3. Jerry Stacks wants to sell hamburgers.   T   F
4. Anna Waleska does not want to change the image of Pizza World.   T   F
5. Anna Waleska wants more American investment in Pizza World.   T   F
6. Jerry Stacks agrees with Anna Waleska's ideas.   T   F

2 What do the following figures refer to?

1. Over a million _____
2. Nearly 300 _____
3. 15 _____
4. 250,000 _____

3 Summarise Anna Waleska's position by putting the words in the box below into the correct places in the text.

fast food   investment   delivery   empty   competition   image   younger

Anna Waleska thinks that Pizza World's restaurants are almost (1) _____ because there is a lot of (2) _____ in Poland from the (3) _____ _____ restaurants. She believes that Pizza World must change its (4) _____ to attract (5) _____ people. She wants to start a home (6) _____ service. But this will mean (7) _____ in scooters.

4 Now put in the missing verbs/contractions in the phrases below.

1. 'Look, _____ wrong, Anna.'
2. 'We _____ _____ over a million…'
3. '… know. But _____ very competitive…'
4. '…Yes, and _____ the second problem.'
5. 'But _____ _____ investment – delivery…'
6. '…simple really, and it _____ _____ much.'
7. 'I _____ _____ what I can do, Anna, but _____ going to be …'

After her meeting with Jerry Stacks, Anna Waleska was optimistic about receiving extra investment from Pizza World, Europe. But three weeks later, she received the following fax:

PIZZA WORLD Europe
99b Kingsway
LONDON WC9 7MP

17 October 19--

Dear Anna

Following our meeting of 26 September, I am sorry to tell you that Pizza World has decided not to invest in a delivery service in Poland. This is not because of the extra cost of scooters and personnel, but we do not want to change our public image. I am sure you will understand our position.

Best regards

Jerry Stacks

Jerry Stacks
Sales Manager, Europe

Anna was very angry, and left Pizza World for a job in a fast food company a few weeks later. Jerry Stacks put the following advertisement in some Polish and European newspapers.

> **A well-known US pizza company is looking for an ambitious person to manage its restaurants in Warsaw and Cracow.**
>
> We want someone:
> - well-qualified (aged 25–35)
> - with restaurant management experience;
> - who speaks good Polish and English;
> - who is free immediately.
>
> If you are interested, please write to:
> Jerry Stacks
> Box Number 123
> London WC9 7MP
>
> Interviews will be held (in English) in Warsaw during the first week of December.

5 *Looking for a job*. Fill in the missing words from the box below.

| selected | letter | experience | curriculum vitae | interview | apply |

Usually it's necessary to (1) _____ for a job by sending a (2) _____ with a (3) _____ explaining that you have the right professional (4) _____ for the job. Then you may be asked to go for an (5) _____. If this is successful, you are (6) _____.

Jerry Stacks received 24 applications. He chose three possible candidates.

	1	2	3
Name	Pauline/Peter Jackson	Magda/Maciek Cybulski	Ulrike/Ulrich Schmidt
Nationality	British	Polish	German
Age	32	29	37
Present job	Manager of Mill Restaurant (London)	Manager of La Belle Epoque (Paris)	Manager of Pizzahaus (Hamburg)
Previous job	Restaurant manager, Munich (Germany)	Wine waiter, Lyon (France)	Restaurant manager, Chicago (US)
Reasons for wanting job	Polish husband/wife	Wants to return to Poland	Many friends in Warsaw
Foreign languages	Some German and Polish	Good French and English	Good Polish (Polish mother) and English
Availability	Now	In 4 months	In 2 months

30

Role plays – Interviews

Work in pairs. One of you is Jerry Stacks, the other, one of the candidates. Before starting, read the notes below:

For Jerry Stacks (the interviewer)

You have lost the candidate's curriculum vitae (but you know his/her name) so you must ask a lot of basic questions.

First, offer coffee and talk about general subjects. Then ask about:
- nationality
- age
- present job
- previous job
- why he/she wants to work for Pizza World
- languages
- when he/she is free to start.

Finally, try to answer any questions he/she asks. But you do *not* want to talk about why the previous manager (Anna Waleska) left Pizza World. And you do *not* want to discuss competition from the fast food companies.

For the candidate

Answer Jerry Stack's questions, then ask:
- why the previous manager left;
- if a pizza home delivery service is planned.

Finally, you have heard that Pizza World has problems in Poland. Ask about them.

Afterwards

1 Following your discussions, you decided to offer the job to: _____
Here is the letter you sent to him/her. Fill in the blanks.

```
                    PIZZA WORLD Europe
                        99b Kingsway
                    LONDON WC9 7MP

                                        16 December 19--

Dear _____ (name of candidate)

(1) _____ your interview last Tuesday, I am (2)
_____ to tell you that your
(3) _____ for the job of Manager of Pizza World
in Poland has been (4) _____. In our opinion, you
have the right (5) _____ for the job, and we
look forward to welcoming you to our (6) _____.
   Regarding (7) _____, we agreed on 3,700
zlotys per month, plus free meals. Please send me a
formal letter of acceptance.

Yours (8) _____

        [signature: Jerry Stacks]

Jerry Stacks
Sales Manager, Europe
```

2 Read the telephone conversation below, then fill in the restaurant manager's questions:

Restaurant manager (RM), Customer (C). The Riverside Restaurant has tables on its outside terrace as well as inside.

RM: Riverside Restaurant, good evening.
C: Hello. I'd like to book a table.
RM: Certainly, madam. _____?
C: The 14th July.
RM: _____ a table on the terrace or inside?
C: On the terrace, please.
RM: Just a minute…. Yes, that's OK. _____?
C: Four.
RM: _____?
C: Eight o'clock.
RM: Eight o'clock. Fine. _____?
C: Jenkins. Mrs Jenkins.
RM: Right. So that's a table for four on the 14th July at 8 o'clock in the name of Mrs Jenkins.
C: Thank you very much. Goodbye.
RM: Goodbye, madam.

UNIT 5 — *Business or Sport?*

Introduction

Did you know that...?

- ...there are about 23 million registered football players in the world.
- ... the final game of the 1998 World Cup had a worldwide television audience of 1.7 billion people.
- ...generalised drugs testing on sports competitors first took place at the Munich Olympics in 1972.

Linking and exchanging

1 Who does what during a football match? Link the people (on the left) to their 'jobs' by drawing lines.

players	are responsible for physical fitness
the referee	try to stop goals
captains	try to score goals
goalkeepers	is responsible for fair play
trainers	lead their teams during the game

Are you interested in football? Who is the captain of your national team? Which local club do you support?

Now link the following famous players to their countries of origin and write in their nationalities:

Player	Country	Nationality
Zinedine Zidane	Britain	_____
Ronaldo	Argentina	_____
Franz Beckenbauer	Italy	_____
Diego Maradona	France	_____
Michael Owen	Germany	_____
Paolo Maldini	Brazil	_____

2 Read the following text.

In the UK, football has increased its popularity in recent years, and the business of football has changed. In the past, it was limited to the merchandising of shirts and scarves etc., which clubs sold to their supporters. But now, especially for the top clubs, two things have changed.

The supporters. According to a recent survey by the Centre for Football Research, the average football supporter is a member of the AB (middle and professional) class.

The sponsors. This has had an effect on the sponsors of football clubs. Now, telecommunications and financial companies are replacing the more traditional sponsors – breweries or local banks.

Now look for words in the text that have the same meaning as the following words and write them in the space provided.

1 risen   _____
2 selling   _____
3 study (noun) _____
4 social category _____
5 beer-making companies _____

3 Circle the best answers to the following statements – TRUE, FALSE, or DON'T KNOW.

1	The standard of football has increased recently.	TRUE/FALSE/DON'T KNOW
2	The popularity of football has decreased.	TRUE/FALSE/DON'T KNOW
3	More professional people watch football.	TRUE/FALSE/DON'T KNOW
4	Brewery sponsors are replacing telecommunications companies.	TRUE/FALSE/DON'T KNOW
5	Players are better paid than before.	TRUE/FALSE/DON'T KNOW

4 Barnfield United is a Second Division club – and it has problems. It has just lost five matches in succession and will be relegated to the Third Division next season.

Reading note: What does *relegated* mean? _____

Now listen to a local radio interview between a sports journalist and Tommy Moore, the manager of Barnfield United.
Fill in the missing words to complete this summary of the interview.

Tommy Moore describes the defeat as a (1) _____ and agrees that there weren't many (2) _____. The journalist says that, without supporters, a football team (3) _____ money. Tommy Moore replies that he must find good players, who score goals, so that Barnfield United will (4) _____ money again. He wants to get a new (5) _____ and new players from (6) _____. He thinks that the team will return to the (7) _____ _____ next year. He has no (8) _____ about the financing of his plans.

GRAMMAR NOTES: RELATIVE PRONOUNS, INTERROGATIVES AND A CONTRACTION

who   which   whose   who's

Read the following sentences.

who: He's the man who hopes to be the next manager.
Who wants to go to the conference?

which: I train a good team which wins matches.
Which is the best rugby team in your country?

whose: That's the club whose trainer resigned last week.
Whose idea was this?

who's: She's a player who's going to succeed.
Who's the best tennis player in your country?

Now put in the correct word.

1 The company _____ got the contract has started work.
2 _____ going to start the meeting?
3 _____ team won, Arsenal or Real Madrid?
4 He's the inspector _____ works for the government.
5 "_____ office is this?" "Marie's."
6 _____ day do you prefer, Monday or Tuesday?
7 That was the company _____ profits fell last year.
8 _____ will meet you in Calcutta?

FUNCTION NOTES

Look at these phrases. They will be useful in the role plays in this unit.

Interrogating:
Tell me, wh…?   I want to know wh…?   I want you to tell me wh… .

Making excuses/justifications:
It wasn't my fault, because… .   I'm sorry, but… .
I didn't mean to …but you see… .   No, that's not true… .

Role plays – Sports problems

ROLE PLAY ONE   A

Name: Carla/Carlos Martinez

You are a doctor. You did a drugs test on Mireille/Mathieu Stefanovitch, a champion swimmer. The test was positive.

Interview him/her. First, tell him/her about the result of the test. You want to know about relations with his/her trainer (who has a bad reputation) and about his/her diet and medicines. After the interview, decide what to do and tell Mireille/Mathieu.

ROLE PLAY ONE   B

You are Mireille/Mathieu Stefanovitch, a champion swimmer. You had a drugs test from Carla/Carlos Martinez, a doctor. You do not know the result of the test. Your trainer is responsible for your diet, and you obey him. Sometimes he gives you tablets before important championships. He says they will help you to relax.

ROLE PLAY TWO — A

You are the trainer for Purley Giants, a volleyball team. You will interview Julia/Julio Spinelli, a well-known player. He/she is very popular with the supporters, but not with the other players. He/she often misses training sessions. You know that he/she likes to go to discos and parties. If this situation does not change, you will drop him/her from the team.

ROLE PLAY TWO — B

Name: Julia/Julio Spinelli

You are a well-known volleyball player with the Purley Giants team. You love volleyball, but you also like discos and parties. You often go to bed at 4.00 a.m. so you cannot wake up in the morning and sometimes miss training sessions. You think the other players are jealous of your popularity. Discuss the situation with your trainer.

ROLE PLAY THREE — A

You are the manager of a national tennis team. You will interview Gundela/Gunther Hayek, one of your best players. But he/she has a bad reputation. Last week he/she insulted an umpire and threw a racket at his/her opponent. You know he/she has personal problems, and was recently divorced. First, ask about the incidents last week, then suggest a rest or some counselling.

ROLE PLAY THREE — B

You are Gundela/Gunther Hayek, a champion tennis player. Your public reputation is not good. Last week you insulted an umpire and threw a racket at your opponent. Also, you were divorced recently.

You say:
- the umpire made a wrong decision;
- your opponent insulted you.

It is the end of the season and you are tired. Discuss your problems with your team manager.

Storyline

Barnfield United – one year later. Three things have changed:
- Barnfield United has a new trainer, Wim Nugteren, from Holland;
- the club bought a young Brazilian, Junio Cabral, for £500,000;
- the club found a new sponsor, Totley Holdings, a London finance company.

Tommy Moore was confident about the future. But things did not improve:
- Wim Nugteren was a popular trainer, and went to night-clubs with the players, but Barnfield United continued to lose matches;
- Junio Cabral was also popular with everybody, but did not score many goals;
- Finally, Barney Frazer, the Director of Totley Holdings, was not happy sponsoring a club which lost matches.

| 36 |

One morning, Tommy Moore received a letter from the Second Division Italian club, Garibaldi Valenzo. Here is an extract:

> **CONFIDENTIAL**
>
> ... so we will offer the equivalent of £350,000 for the transfer of Junio Cabral at the beginning of next season. Please think about this offer and let us have your reaction.
>
> Yours sincerely
>
> *Gianni Pavese*
>
> Gianni Pavese
> Manager, Garibaldi Valenzo

1 Tommy Moore immediately asked to see Wim Nugteren. Listen to their conversation and circle the best answers to the following.

1 Wim Nugteren thinks the offer from Garibaldi Valenzo is (a) too high.
(b) too low.

2 Junio Cabral (a) does not like the climate in the UK.
(b) likes the climate in the UK.

3 The supporters of Barnfield United (a) prefer British players.
(b) like Junio Cabral.

4 It is (a) Wim Nugteren's fault that Barnfield is in the Third Division.
(b) Junio Cabral's fault that Barnfield is in the Third Division.

5 Wim Nugteren is (a) a good trainer. (b) friendly with the players.

6 Tommy Moore has (a) not yet decided about Junio Cabral's future.
(b) already decided about Junio Cabral's future.

2 Near the end of the conversation, Tommy Moore gave three instructions to improve discipline among the players. What were the details?

1 Training sessions: _____

2 Salaries: _____

3 Night-clubs: _____

3 What do the following figures refer to?

1 £350,000: _____

2 5: _____

3 15%: _____

4 £25: _____

4 Fill in the missing words.

1 '... for a player _____ doesn't like...'

2 'But _____ fault is that?'

3 'You're the man _____ responsible for...'

Tommy Moore decided to have a meeting to discuss the situation. He invited the following people:

Wim Nugteren, the trainer
Barney Frazer, of Totley Holdings
The supporters' representative

The players' representative
Junio Cabral's lawyer

5 Business or Sport? © Delta Publishing 1998

Role play – What future for a football star?

ROLE ONE

You are Tommy Moore, Chairman of the meeting. You want:
- to continue the Totley Holdings sponsorship;
- to keep the Barnfield United supporters.

You are still *undecided* about the future of Junio Cabral, but you think it is time to drop Wim Nugteren. Barnfield United has no money.

ROLE TWO

You are Wim Nugteren, the trainer. You want:
- to refuse Garibaldi Valenzo's offer (Junio Cabral's playing is improving – he scored two goals last Saturday).

You agree that the team needs more discipline.

ROLE THREE

You are Barney Frazer of Totley Holdings. You want:
- to accept Garibaldi Valenzo's offer (Junio Cabral was not a good investment);
- to drop Wim Nugteren (the team needs a new trainer).

If Tommy Moore does not agree to these conditions, Totley Holdings will stop sponsorship.

ROLE FOUR

You are the supporters' representative. You want:
- to keep Junio Cabral (he is popular, and scored two goals last Saturday);
- to drop Wim Nugteren and find a new trainer.

ROLE FIVE

You are the players' representative. You want:
- to accept Garibaldi Valenzo's offer (some of the players are jealous of Junio Cabral's popularity);
- to keep Wim Nugteren (he is popular with the players).

ROLE SIX

You are Junio Cabral's lawyer. You want:
- £500,000 for his transfer to Garibaldi Valenzo;
- plus a special payment of £25,000 (because Junio Cabral's contract was for three years, so he will lose money if he leaves Barnfield United now).

Junio Cabral wants to go to Italy because the climate is better.

Afterwards

1 Following what you decided in the meeting, complete this newspaper interview between a journalist and Tommy Moore. Then complete the final paragraph of the newspaper article in the same way.

'Well, Tommy, I hear there will be changes at Barnfield United.'

'Yes. First of all, team discipline. We have decided to _____
_____
_____

'Does this affect the future of your trainer, Wim Nugteren?'

'Yes. He _____
_____

'And what about sponsorship from Totley Holdings?'

'Well, Totley Holdings have decided to _____
_____

'And the most important point. Can you say anything about the future of Junio Cabral?'

'Yes. He will _____
_____

'Can you give me any financial details?'

'No. I have no comment on our finances.'

The final paragraph of the article was:

'Mr Moore had no comment on the financial details, but I have heard that _____
_____
_____
_____

2 Do you practise a sport? If you do, write about it, saying:
- which sport you practise
- where and how often you play it
- if it is a team sport (like football) or an individual sport (like swimming)
- why you like it.

Or: You probably have a favourite sport that you watch on TV. Write a few sentences about:
- what it is
- who its champions are
- the team you support
- why you like it.

Or: If you do not like sports, write down your reasons. Do you dislike all sports, or just some in particular?

UNIT 6　　　　　*Slot-Machine Food*

Introduction

Did you know that...?

- ...the first 'vending machine' was probably invented in Ancient Egypt around 200 BC. It was used to sell holy water in an Egyptian temple.
- ... the first vending machines of the twentieth century sold stamps, cigarettes and chewing gum.
- ...modern vending machines have refrigeration or heating for their products, and there are now over six million machines in the US alone.

Linking and exchanging

1 *Staff restaurants* (also called staff canteens). Read the following two texts then fill in the missing words from the box below:

☺

'Our staff restaurant's very good. The food is always _____ and the salads are _____. There's a different _____ every day and the tables are _____. Also, we have a coffee _____ next to the restaurant with a separate _____ section.'

☹

'Our staff restaurant's terrible! There's always a long _____ and there are never enough _____ , so some people have to carry their _____ . The knives and forks are often _____ and it's very _____, so conversation's difficult. What's more, the food's _____!'

noisy	fresh	menu	non-smoking	queue	hot	clean
	trays	bar	plates	cold	dirty	

2 *Comprehension*. Two employees of a British company – Danny and Mike – are having lunch in their staff restaurant. Listen to their conversation then choose the best answers to the following questions.

1. There are (a) a lot of people in the staff restaurant.
    (b) not a lot of people in the staff restaurant.
2. Mike's sausages are (a) not well-cooked.
    (b) well-cooked.
3. The staff restaurant (a) will close.
    (b) is going to be sold.
4. Danny says that in the staff restaurant (a) it's possible to relax.
    (b) people cannot relax.
5. Mike says vending machines (a) take a lot of space.
    (b) are efficient.

3 *Adjectives and their opposites*. Mike thinks vending machines are efficient and hygienic, but Danny doesn't agree.
Look at the following 'positive' adjectives, and write their *opposites* by adding the prefixes: **in-**, **un-** or **im-**.

1. efficient _____
2. personal _____
3. pleasant _____
4. friendly _____
5. effective _____
6. practical _____
7. suitable _____
8. convenient _____

Role plays – Is compromise possible?

ROLE PLAY ONE   A
With your partner, you are planning the end-of-year office party. You want to visit a discothèque. Most of your colleagues are young and they like dancing.

ROLE PLAY ONE   B
With your partner, you are planning the end-of-year office party. You want to go to a restaurant. You are sure that the senior managers do not like discothèques.

ROLE PLAY ONE
Possible compromise: a buffet dinner in the company conference room with disco music.

ROLE PLAY TWO   A
You are the Chief Executive of a large company. The company has a holiday home beside the sea for the children of its employees. But the holiday home is very expensive to operate and you have decided to close it. Tell your partner, who is the Personnel Manager.

ROLE PLAY TWO   B
You are the Personnel Manager of a large company. The company has a holiday home beside the sea for the children of its employees. Every summer approximately 100 children stay at the home during school holidays. It is very popular and not expensive. Your partner is the Chief Executive of the company.

ROLE PLAY TWO

Possible compromises:
- raise the prices;
- use the holiday home for management training;
- rent the holiday home to other companies.

ROLE PLAY THREE — A/B

The offices in your company are not very attractive. The paint on the walls is very dirty. The desks and chairs are uncomfortable and the carpets are old. There are many windows, so it is too hot in the summer. There are no flowers or plants. You have a budget of £15,000 to redecorate your offices.

Look at these costs:
- repaint the walls (£8,000);
- buy new desks and chairs (£10,000);
- buy new carpets (£5,000);
- install sunblinds (£5,000)
- buy plants and flowers (£2,000).

Now, with your partner, discuss what to do.

ROLE PLAY THREE — A

You are very practical. You want to buy new desks and chairs and install sunblinds.

ROLE PLAY THREE — B

You are interested in the appearance of the offices. You want to repaint the walls, buy some plants and flowers and buy new carpets.

ROLE PLAY THREE

Possible compromise:
- repaint walls;
- install sunblinds;
- buy plants and flowers.

GRAMMAR NOTES: PREPOSITIONS OF PLACE

Ustensilas do Brasil manufactures high quality cooking materials (saucepans etc). Look at the site plan below, and choose the right prepositions from the box.

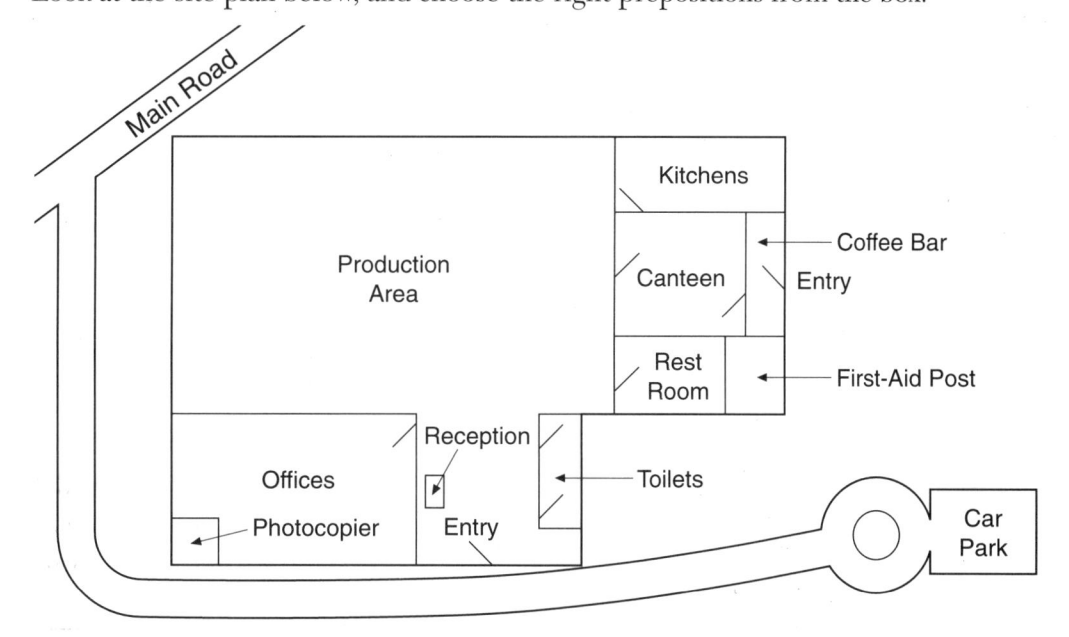

6 Slot-Machine Food © Delta Publishing 1998

| opposite | on | beside | between | to | behind |

1. The toilets are _____ the right.
2. The offices are _____ the left.
3. The photocopier is diagonally _____ the door.
4. The canteen is _____ the kitchens and the rest room.
5. The kitchens are _____ the canteen.
6. The coffee bar is _____ the canteen.

Other prepositions of place are: **near**, **next to**, **in front of**

How can you use them to describe the site plan?

FUNCTIONS/SKILLS NOTES: ASKING FOR AND GIVING DIRECTIONS

Look at these expressions.

Asking: 'Where is the X, please?'
'How do I get to the X, please?'
'Is this the way to the X, please?'

Giving: 'You take the first/second turning on the left/right…'
'You go straight on until you come to…'
'… and the X is on your left/right/just in front of you.'

Work in pairs, using the site plan of Ustensilas do Brasil.

1. You are on the main road. Ask your partner to direct you to the offices.
2. You are in the reception area. Ask your partner to direct you to the coffee bar.
3. You are in the car park. Ask your partner to direct you to the toilets.
4. You are in the rest room. Ask your partner to direct you to the main road.

Storyline

Ustensilas do Brasil was recently bought by a Swedish company, Copperbottom, based in Stockholm. Lars Petersson, the Managing Director, sent this e-mail to Antonio da Costa, the Production Manager of Ustensilas do Brasil.

1. Read the e-mail, then answer the True/False questions that follow. Circle the correct answer.

> Hi Antonio,
>
> I've got a job for you. Do you know that in your factory, the kitchen, the canteen and the coffee bar take up nearly 30% of your total space (900 square metres)? I think this is far too much. So before my visit next month, can you prepare plans for vending machines and a stand-only coffee bar (50 square metres max.)? By the way, this is confidential. Don't want to start trouble, do we?
>
> Thanks
>
> Lars

1	The present staff canteen is 50 metres square.	TRUE	FALSE
2	Lars Petersson thinks this is too small.	TRUE	FALSE
3	He wants to expand the production area.	TRUE	FALSE
4	He will bring expansion plans to Brazil.	TRUE	FALSE
5	He wants to put chairs in the coffee bar.	TRUE	FALSE

2 It is a month later. Lars Petersson has arrived in Brazil, and Antonio da Costa has prepared a plan for expanding the production area.

He describes the plan to Lars Petersson and the managers of Ustensilas do Brasil. First, listen to the description and fill in A and B below.

A – extra production area: _____

B – cost of plan: _____

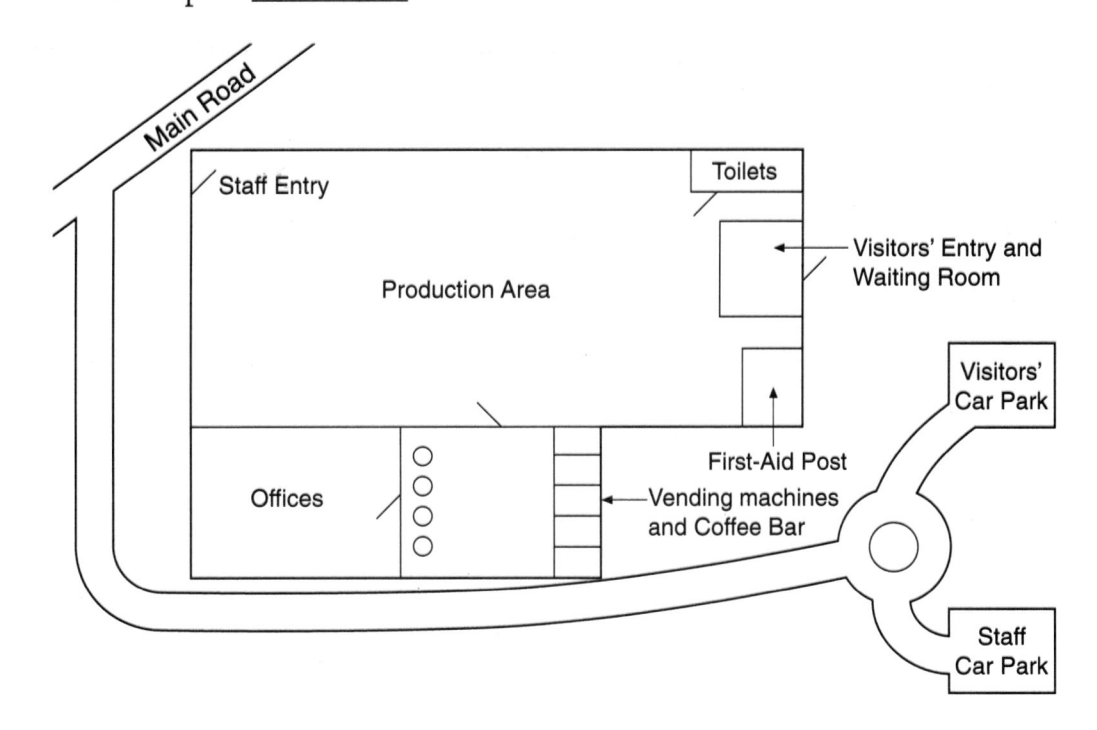

3 Now listen again and fill in the missing prepositions from the text below:

The vending machines will be put (1) _____ the offices and the visitors' entry will be (2) _____ the toilets and the first-aid post. The car park will be (3) _____ the new entry. The office staff will be (4) _____ the vending machines, but they won't be very (5) _____ the toilets.

4 The *advantages* of the plan are: a _____
b _____
c _____

The *disadvantages* of the plan are: d _____
e _____
f _____

Look at the plan carefully. Can you see other advantages or disadvantages from:
- the management's viewpoint?
- the staff's viewpoint?

6 Slot-Machine Food   © Delta Publishing 1998

Role play – Goodbye, canteen?

As Maria Silva predicted, the plan was not popular with the staff. So Lars Petersson decided to have a meeting with their representatives.

ROLE ONE

You are Lars Petersson, Chairperson of the meeting. Begin by explaining the plan. Then ask for opinions. The plan will make the company more competitive. You will be able to buy new machines.

ROLE TWO

You are Antonio da Costa. Your plan will help production, save time and result in better profits (and higher salaries).

ROLE THREE

You are Maria Silva, the Personnel Manager. You do not like the plan. Can you think of a compromise solution (for example, a smaller self-service canteen in the present entry hall)? Note down other possible compromises.

ROLE FOUR

You are the representative of the production staff. You are against vending machines. Suggest expanding the present production area towards the main road.

ROLE FIVE

You are the representative of the office staff. You do not want vending machines near the offices (problems of noise). Also, the new staff entry is too far from the staff car park.

ROLE SIX

You are the Canteen Manager. The staff like your canteen, and the meals are cheap. You have worked for Ustensilas do Brasil or 23 years. Note down other arguments in favour of keeping the staff canteen.

Afterwards

1 Here is the beginning of a text summarising the decisions of your meeting. First, draw a site plan below of what you agreed:

[Site plan area with "Main Road" labelled diagonally in the upper left corner]

Now describe it in writing, using the correct prepositions. (Remember to include: visitors' car park/staff entry/toilets/staff entry etc.)

'At a meeting between management and staff representatives last week, we decided that vending machines _____

_____

_____

_____

_____

_____

2 Cash dispensing machines at banks are a part of modern life. We use them every day. But how? Put the verbs in the box in the correct places in the following instructions:

| wait | insert | press | enter | choose | take | retrieve |

First, _____ your bank card. Then _____ your personal code and _____ the validation button. _____ the amount of money you want and _____ for a few seconds. _____ your card and _____ your banknote(s) and your receipt.

Have you ever entered the wrong code? What happened?

Which statement do you agree with, and why?
'Cash dispensing machines are impersonal. I prefer to visit my bank.'
'Cash dispensing machines are useful. I can get money when I like.'

6 Slot-Machine Food   © Delta Publishing 1998

UNIT 7 *Supermarkets or Shops?*

Introduction

Did you know that…?

- …butchers have lost a third of their trade and grocery shops a quarter of their trade in the last seven years.
- …in the UK the number of supermarkets increased from 10 in 1949 to 4,764 in 1997.
- …sales of organic food in the UK are increasing by 25% a year.

Linking and exchanging

1 *Supermarkets and shops – their differences.* Link the following verbs and noun phrases to make logical sentences. Write the correct numbers in the box provided.

1 Supermarkets
2 Shopkeepers
3 Customers can pay
4 In supermarkets
5 Shops

1 by credit card
2 there are often queues
3 are usually cheaper
4 close earlier
5 give personal service

1 at the check-out.
2 than supermarkets.
3 to their customers.
4 than shops.
5 in supermarkets.

1	2	3	4	5

Where do you prefer to go shopping – in a supermarket or a shop?

GRAMMAR NOTES: TRENDS AND PREPOSITIONS WITH NUMBERS

When we describe the 'movement' of numerical information, we use specific terms.

For *upward* movement (↗)

Verbs	Nouns
to go up	–
to rise	a rise
to increase	an increase

For *downward* movement (↘)

Verbs	Nouns
to go down	–
to fall	a fall
to decrease	a decrease

It is important to use the right **preposition** when describing the movement of numbers. For example:

Profits increased *from* two *to* four thousand dollars.
Sales went down *by* 20 per cent.
Sales stood *at* £3,000 per week.
Profits were *between* £50 *and* £65 a day in 1997.

Warbury is a small town in the north of England. In 1985, Mary Flanagan opened a shop which sold books and stationery (paper, envelopes, pens, etc.). And in 1987, James Penrose opened a supermarket which sold meat, fruit and vegetables. For some years, Mary and James made good profits – and were friends. Then, in 1995, James also began to sell stationery (as well as books and compact discs). His prices were 15% lower than Mary's, and the supermarket was open on Sunday mornings. Mary's sales began to fall. Look at this graph of her profits between 1992 and now:

MARY FLANAGAN – PROFITS ON SALES

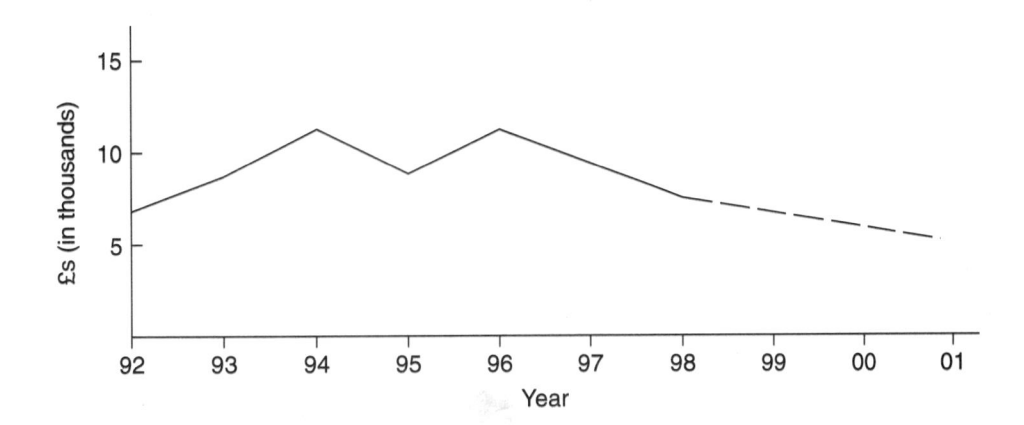

2 Mary Flanagan was very concerned, so she asked for advice from her accountant, Adam Bales. Listen to their conversation and answer the questions below.

Put in the correct signs (↗, △, ↘) and words to describe Mary's profits from 1992 to now.

		Sign	Word(s)
1	1992	X	_____
2	1993	____	_____
3	1994	____	_____
4	1995	____	_____
5	1996	____	_____
6	1997	____	_____
7	now	____	_____

3 *Comprehension.*

1. What happened to the supermarket in 1996? _____
2. What was James Penrose's reaction? _____
3. What was the effect on Mary's profits? _____

4 *Numerical information.* What do the following figures refer to?

1. 'fifteen to twelve thousand pounds' _____
2. 'two months' _____
3. 'three thousand' _____

5 *Discussion.* Mary's last question to her accountant was, 'What can I do, Adam?' What do you think?

For example, she can:
- lower her prices;
- make special promotions;
- advertise in the newspapers;
- distribute free pens.

Your idea(s):

- _____
- _____

6 Now write a short description of the graph below, which shows the profits of James Penrose's supermarket last year.

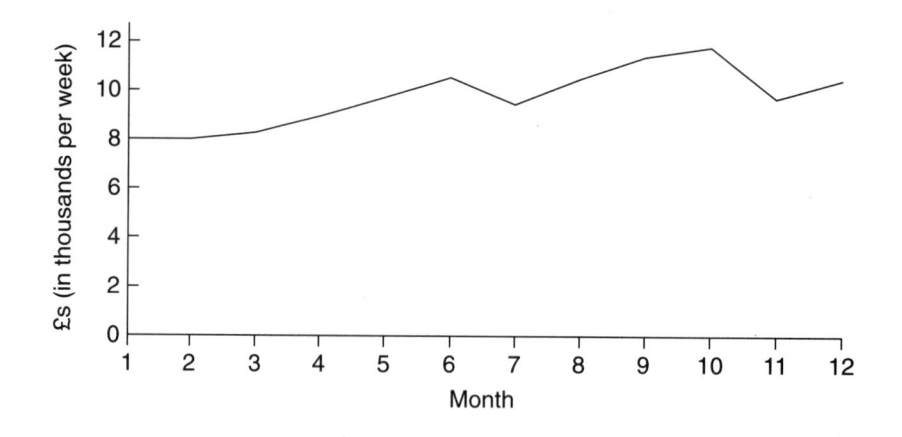

James Penrose had a good year. At the beginning of Month 1 (January), his profits were £8,000 per week. Then _____

_____
_____
_____
_____
_____
_____

7 Supermarkets or Shops? © Delta Publishing 1998

SKILLS NOTES: ASKING QUESTIONS (PAST AND PRESENT)

There are many ways of asking questions. Sometimes they are **direct**:
Where does she work? When did he leave the company?

But we also use the **indirect** form:
Can/Could you tell me where she works?
I'd like to/I want to know when he left the company.

Now put the following direct questions into their indirect form:

1 How does he travel to work?   Can you tell me _____
2 Which system did they use?   I want to know _____
3 Why did you leave your last job? I'd like to know _____
4 When does the meeting start?   Could you tell me _____
5 Why does she want a transfer?   I'd like to know _____

Storyline

Market Organics is a British company based in Hampshire (in central southern England). It was founded in 1978 by Sharon Mitchell and her partner, Jeff Jarvis. It produces organic fruits and vegetables. At present, it supplies only the high-class food shops of towns in the south of England. But the market is nearly saturated, so Sharon Mitchell wants to expand into supermarkets.

1 Link the following words to their meanings by drawing lines.

founded	sells to
organic	enlarge
supplies	established
saturated	full
expand	naturally-produced

(**Note**: 'Organic' food is produced without using chemicals, such as insecticides, etc.)

Expansion into supermarkets will not be easy. Market Organics's fruit and vegetables are expensive – perhaps too expensive for supermarket customers.

2 *Comprehension*. Listen to a radio interview between Sharon Mitchell and Lenny Graft, a journalist from the 'Hampshire Morning Business' programme. Answer the following questions by choosing (a) or (b) to complete the sentence.

1 Market Organics wants to sell in supermarkets because:
   (a) food shops are too expensive.
   (b) there are no more possibilities in food shops.

2 Sharon Mitchell wants to:
   (a) stop selling in food shops.
   (b) make her business larger.

3 Sharon Mitchell thinks that:
   (a) people want to buy quality food.
   (b) supermarkets will not sell quality food.

4 Lenny Graft asks if Market Organics's prices are:
   (a) too high for supermarkets.   (b) too high for food shops.

5 Sharon Mitchell wants to:
   (a) advertise on television first.   (b) spend money on radio advertising.

3 *Agreeing and disagreeing*. Fill in Sharon's missing words below:

1 '... high-class food shops.'

'_____ _____. It wasn't easy...'

2 '...too expensive for supermarkets?'

'_____ _____ _____ _____ _____ _____ all.'

3 '... too ambitious?'

'Too ambitious? _____ _____ _____.'

4 During the interview, Lenny Graft mentioned three main difficulties. What did he say about?

a Price: _____

b Size of Market Organics: _____

c Advertising: _____

Role play – A meeting

After her radio interview, Sharon Mitchell was very enthusiastic about selling to supermarkets. First, she made some calculations.

Last year	
Turnover	£500,000
Salaries	£250,000
Transport	£42,000
Advertising	£10,000
Packaging	£10,000
Other costs	£140,000
Profit	£48,000
Extra cost of selling to supermarkets (forecast)	
Transport & packaging	£60,000
Extra sales staff	£40,000
Advertising	£10,000

Then she arranged a meeting with the following people:
- Jeff Jarvis, her business partner
- the Distribution Manager of Market Organics
- the Marketing Manager of Market Organics
- an Advertising Consultant
- her Bank Manager

During the meeting, the participants must decide if Market Organics will sell to supermarkets or not. The problems to discuss are:

If they sell to supermarkets
- transport
- new packaging
- advertising
- bank loan
- lower prices

If they do not sell to supermarkets
- other outlets
- future sales
- higher prices

7 Supermarkets or Shops?   © Delta Publishing 1998

ROLE ONE

You are Sharon Mitchell, Chairperson of the meeting. Plan the meeting carefully. Begin by describing the present situation of Market Organics, then ask for opinions. Make a note of the decisions of the meeting.
(You want a bank loan of £100,000.)

ROLE TWO

You are Jeff Jarvis, Sharon's business partner. You are *against* supermarket distribution.
(You think it is bad for the image of Market Organics.)

ROLE THREE

You are the Distribution Manager. At present, you have only two lorries. Distribution to supermarkets will be impossible.
(Need three extra lorries – cost £40,000.)

ROLE FOUR

You are the Marketing Manager. In your opinion, supermarket customers will not pay high prices for quality food.
(Prices must be lowered by 20%. Packaging must be changed – cost £15,000.)

ROLE FIVE

You are the Advertising Consultant. You are in favour of supermarket distribution. You advise a television advertising campaign.
(Cost £55,000.)

ROLE SIX

You are the Bank Manager. You think Market Organics will need more staff and transport possibilities to sell to supermarkets. You prefer limited supermarket outlets with newspaper advertising only.
(Bank loan limit – £50,000.)

7 Supermarkets or Shops?   © Delta Publishing 1998
This page may be photocopied under the terms outlined on p.ii.

Afterwards

1 What did you decide? Write a report of the meeting to be sent to all participants. Give reasons/explanations for your decisions – especially those related to transport, packaging and advertising costs.

Meeting: Selling to supermarkets
Date: 15 July 19--

At the meeting to discuss the future of Market Organics, it was decided that:

1 _____
_____
_____

2 _____
_____
_____

3 _____
_____
_____

4 _____
_____
_____

---

2 *Developing arguments*. Choose one (or more) of the following statements and develop it in writing. Some key words/phrases are given to help you:

1 Small shops are important to the life of a town.
   (***Key words/phrases*** – human contact/quality of goods and service/people without cars/older people/community)

2 The future is in supermarkets.
   (***Key words/phrases*** – low prices/wide choice/efficiency/opening and closing times/credit cards)

3 Supermarkets are dangerous in the long term.
   (***Key words/phrases*** – end of small shops/poor quality/aggressive selling/often no choice of supermarket/transport problems)

UNIT 8 — *Choosing a Supplier*

Introduction

What is a department store? Do you have them in your country? How many can you name?

Did you know that…?

> Department stores began in the 19th century. The first was Bon Marché, established in Paris in 1838. Printemps, also in Paris, was founded in 1885 and sells many products – from perfume to tableware. There are now 19 Printemps department stores in France, which employ about 5,000 people. Clothes represent 41% of total sales.

Linking and exchanging

1 Read the following text. Do you know the underlined words? Write what you think they mean in the space below.

The <u>fashion</u> industry is very competitive, so <u>designers</u> and <u>manufacturers</u> must be <u>up-to-date</u>. But for department stores, quality is also important. If the colours of a dress <u>fade</u> after only a month, the customer will <u>complain</u>. So <u>buyers</u> for department stores are very careful about choosing the <u>suppliers</u>.

fashion	_____	fade	_____
designers	_____	complain	_____
manufacturers	_____	buyers	_____
up-to-date	_____	suppliers	_____

2 Link the verbs with their adjectives and nouns to make correct sentences.

Department store buyers have an interesting job. They often travel to foreign countries. And if they work for the Fashion Department of a store, they must:

choose	good English.
negotiate	reliable suppliers.
speak	the lowest prices.
attend	the important fashion shows.

3 *Pairwork.* What are the qualities of a good department store assistant? First, put the suggestions below in order of priority (adding any of your own).

____ smart clothes   ____ good education

____ patience   ____ humour

____ knowledge of product   ____ _____

____ politeness   ____ _____

Now compare your answers with your partner's. Do you agree?

GRAMMAR NOTES: COMPARISONS AND REGULAR ADJECTIVES

When we make comparisons between two elements, we add '*...er than*' to short adjectives and '*more ... than*' or '*less ... than*' to long adjectives.

When talking about superlatives, we add '*the ...est*' to short adjectives and '*the most ...*' or '*the least ...*' to long adjectives. For example:

Inhabitants (millions)

ARGENTINA	BRAZIL	ITALY
32	158	58

(Adjectives: *large   populated*)

Italy's population is *larger than* Argentina's, but Brazil's is *the largest*.

Italy is *more populated than* Argentina, but *less populated than* Brazil.

Brazil is *the most populated* and Argentina *the least populated* of the three countries.

Be careful – some adjectives are irregular.

Choose the correct comparative or superlative form of the adjectives in *italics* in the text below:

Aberdash is the (1) *most big/biggest/bigger* department store in our town. It offers a (2) *more wide/most wide/wider* choice than the others and it is (3) *more profitable/least profitable/profitabler* than Fashionmart, its main competitor. Also, the clothes at Aberdash are (4) *most expensive/less expensive/expensivest* and its employees are (5) *more professional/professionaler/least professional*.

FUNCTIONS/SKILLS NOTES: AGREEING AND DISAGREEING

When native English speakers discuss problems, they use very simple expressions to give opinions, agree and disagree. For example:

Giving an opinion: 'I think…'
Agreeing: 'Yes' or 'OK'
Disagreeing: 'Yes, but…'

But in *international* meetings, it's necessary to be more precise. Link the following expressions to the verbs in the box below:

believe	agree	go	disagree	think

1 Yes, I _____ with you.
2 What do you _____ about that?
3 In principle, I _____ along with you, but…
4 I'm sorry, I _____ completely.
5 Personally, I _____ we must…

Storyline

BONPRIX is a large department store in Paris with 860 employees. Françoise Bernardon is the Chief Buyer for women's clothes and accessories (handbags, belts etc.). HAMMAT FABRICS is a supplier of women's clothes, mainly summer dresses and skirts. Recently, there have been complaints about Hammat's products.

1 Listen to the following conversation between a customer and a sales assistant at Bonprix.

  1 When did the customer buy the dress? _____
  2 What has happened to it? _____
  3 What does the sales assistant ask for? _____
  4 What does she offer to do? _____
  5 What does the customer want? _____

Role plays – Complaining

ROLE PLAY ONE   A

You have just returned from a holiday in a holiday village in the south of France. The tourist brochure said: • lunch included • free wine with dinner • family chalets.

But 'lunch' was a sandwich, the 'free wine' was undrinkable and you shared your chalet with another family. Go and see the travel agent and complain.

You want: a 50% refund.

ROLE PLAY ONE   B

You are a travel agent, specialising in low-price holidays to the south of France. One of your clients will come to complain.

Explain that:
- the brochure did not specify what type of lunch;
- you cannot hope for fine wines in a holiday village;
- you are surprised about the chalet, and will investigate the problem.

You cannot promise any refund until you have checked.

---

8 Choosing a Supplier   © Delta Publishing 1998

> ### ROLE PLAY TWO   A
> Recently you bought an expensive (but complicated) alarm clock from a shop. But it doesn't work, and last week you missed an international meeting. Because of this, your company lost an important contract. Go and see the shop manager. You want a refund.

> ### ROLE PLAY TWO   B
> You are the manager of a shop. You sell alarm clocks and watches. One of your customers will come in to complain. You think that he/she did not regulate the alarm clock correctly (it is complicated). Your shop does not give refunds.

> ### ROLE PLAY THREE   A
> You are an airline pilot. You work irregular hours and live in an apartment. Your neighbour plays his guitar late at night, and you cannot sleep. If this continues, you will be a danger to your passengers. Go and speak to your neighbour.

> ### ROLE PLAY THREE   B
> You are a professional musician. You live in an apartment and work irregular hours. Usually you practise at home, during the night. But your neighbours are not happy about this. One of them will come and see you. Try to agree on an arrangement with him/her.

There were several more complaints about Hammat's products so when the Director of Hammat (Oliver Jakhri) visited France, Françoise Bernardon met him to discuss the situation.

Listen to their conversation and answer the questions below.

2   **1**   Françoise Bernardon has two complaints about Hammat's dresses. What are they?

    a _____

    b _____

  2   What does she say about the first complaint?

    _____

  3   What is Oliver Jakhri's reaction to the second complaint?

    _____

  4   What does Françoise Bernardon want? Fill in the missing words.

    a   _____ quality

    b   _____ _____ delivery

    c   _____ prices

  5   What did Françoise Bernardon mean when she said, 'There are *other* suppliers, Mr Jakhri.'?

3 How would you describe Françoise Bernardon's attitude?

| aggressive | friendly | angry | understanding | polite |

Oliver Jakhri is in a difficult situation. What would you do in his position?

4 *Pairwork.* With a partner, write an *end* to their conversation. Here are some ideas:
- Promise to improve quality.
- Guarantee delivery dates.
- Drop prices by 5%.
- Invite Françoise Bernardon to lunch.

Role play – Which supplier?

After her conversation with Oliver Jakhri, Françoise Bernardon thought about alternatives. She had two choices:

- to continue to work with Hammat Fabrics; or
- to look for another supplier (there were two possibilities). She noted the following details about each choice.

	1	2	3
Name	Hammat Fabrics	Darlac Fashions	Dawn Dresses
Country	Egypt	Vietnam	Turkey
Distribution	Sea/land	Air/land	Land
Reputation	Normally good, but recent problems with quality and delivery.	Good quality, but delivery needs improving.	Good delivery; not known in France.
Already supplies	France, Italy and Britain	USA and Australasia	Europe, especially Germany

Françoise Bernardon decided to have a meeting to discuss alternative suppliers. Before the meeting, she gave a copy of her notes (above) to the other managers of Bonprix.

ROLE ONE

You are Françoise Bernardon, Purchasing Manager and Chairperson of the meeting. Begin by summarising the situation. Then ask for opinions. You have not yet decided what to do.

ROLE TWO

You are the Sales Manager. You favour Dawn Dresses. Your German colleague says they are efficient. Also, Turkey has associations with the European Union.

ROLE THREE

You are the Distribution Manager. You favour Dawn Dresses for geographical reasons.

ROLE FOUR

You are the Customer Services Manager. You favour Hammat Fabrics. You have known Oliver Jakhri for ten years – he is a friend. You think his difficulties are only temporary.

ROLE FIVE

You are the Quality Manager. You favour Darlac Fashions, but you are uncertain. You want to visit their factory in Vietnam to check on quality. Also, most Vietnamese business people speak French.

ROLE SIX

You are the Finance Manager. You favour Hammat Fabrics because of their reputation. Your second choice is Darlac Fashions because of the very low cost of labour in Vietnam.

Afterwards

1 Françoise Bernardon wrote to Oliver Jakhri the next day. In the first paragraph, choose one of the words/phrases in *italics* that best reflects the decision made during your meeting. If your decision was something different, add your own words/phrases in the spaces provided. In the second paragraph, choose the correct word.

Dear Mr Jakhri,

Following our meeting last week, I am _____/*pleased/sorry* to tell you that Bonprix has decided to _____/*terminate/extend* your contract _____/*until December/in July*. As I told you, we have had several _____/*complaints/compliments* about your products, _____/*so this extension will be reviewed next year/but termination will not be final*.

So please send me your prices for next year, and I hope they will be at least 15% *lowest/lower/more low* than at present.

I look forward to our continued business relationship under *gooder/better/best* conditions.

Yours sincerely,
Françoise Bernardon

---

2 You are an international supplier of one of the main exports of your country. Decide what it is – it can be a product or a service. Next month you will go to the UK to visit several potential British buyers. Now write an introductory letter, using the form below.

Dear Sir or Madam,

As one of the main international suppliers of _____ [your product or service] from _____ [your country], I will be visiting the UK next month and would like to meet you to discuss possibilities.

I have pleasure in enclosing our company brochure. As you can see, our company...

Now continue in your own words, describing:
- the advantages of your product
- its competitive price
- delivery conditions
- where you already sell
- why it would sell well in the UK

and add any of your own ideas.

_____
_____
_____
_____
_____
_____
_____

Yours faithfully,
_____ [your name]

UNIT 9 *Closing a Hospital*

Introduction

Did you know that...?

> ... the number of inhabitants per doctor is very different depending on the country. Look at these statistics:
>
> | | | | | |
> |---|---|---|---|---|
> | Hungary | – 306 | | Columbia | – 1105 |
> | Egypt | – 1310 | | Cuba | – 275 |
> | Gabon | – 1985 | | China | – 1060 |
>
> In the European Union there are also large differences. For instance, Greece (with about 11 million inhabitants) has a doctor/patient ratio of 4.3/1000, while the UK (with about 59 million inhabitants) has a doctor/patient ratio of 2.2/1000.

Have you had much experience of hospitals
– as a patient?
– as a visitor?

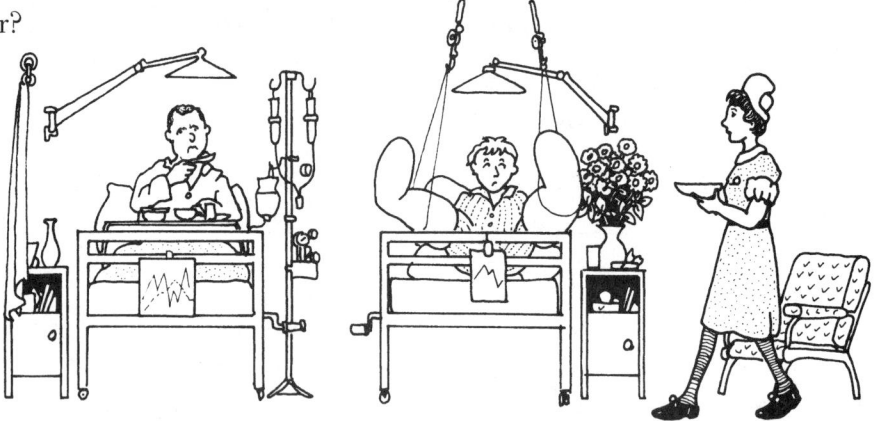

Linking and exchanging

1 *Health services.* Put the words from the box below into the following text.

operation	nurses	general practitioner	examination	anaesthetic

If you are ill, you go and see your _____ first. If he/she thinks it is necessary, you will go to a hospital for an _____. Perhaps you will need an _____. In that case, you will be given an _____ to make you sleep. During your time in hospital, _____ will look after you.

2 *Hospital departments and categories of patients.* Look at the words on the left, then link them to the words on the right by drawing lines.

obstetrics	children
geriatrics	babies
paediatrics	accidents
casualty	old people

3 Which sentences are true *in your country*?
1. There are a lot of local hospitals, and the standard is good.
2. There are many good hospitals in the major cities, but not in the small towns.
3. There are not many specialised (e.g. maternity) hospitals in small towns.
4. We need more geriatric hospitals.
5. The government has no money for the health services.

4 *Pairwork*. Life expectancy and retirement ages in the UK.
Notes: *life expectancy* – the age when most men die.
retirement – the age when most men stop working.

Ask your partner questions to complete your table.

A

Life expectancy for men		Retirement age for men	
Year	**Age**	**Year**	**Age**
1900		1900	age of death
1950	66	1950	
1997		1997	65
2015	105?	2015	

Ask your partner questions to complete your table.

B

Life expectancy for men		Retirement age for men	
Year	**Age**	**Year**	**Age**
1900	59	1900	age of death
1950		1950	70
1997	73	1997	
2015		2015	50?

5 Listen to part of a television interview with Jackie Palmer, a politician. Then summarise what she says by filling in the gaps below.

Jackie Palmer says retired people are living (1) _____ and need health services near their (2) _____. But the government is (3) _____ a lot of hospitals to (4) _____ money. She believes this is (5) _____.

6 *Numbers*. What did the following numbers refer to?
a 60 refers to _____
b 25 refers to _____
c 80 refers to _____

Role plays – Radio interviews

> **ROLE PLAY ONE** A
>
> You are a journalist. You will interview your partner, a local politician. There is a serious problem of drug abuse among the unemployed young people in your town.
> You think:
> • that prison is bad for drug users;
> • that the government must create jobs in the town.

ROLE PLAY ONE   B

You are a local politician. You think the drug problem among the young people of your town is the fault of parents.

You want:
- to put a 10 p.m. curfew on all people under 21;
- to put all drug users in prison;
- young people to go to the city to find jobs.

ROLE PLAY TWO   A

You are a journalist. You will interview your partner, a national politician. His/her political party supports state schools and is against private education. (In your country, only the children of rich parents go to private schools.)

Ask your partner:
- about his/her opinions on state education;
- where his/her children go to school;
- if he/she has any conflicts of interest.

ROLE PLAY TWO   B

You are a national politician. Your political party supports state schools and is against private education.

You:
- think the standard of state education is good;
- send your children to an expensive private school;
- are a paid director of a well-known private school.

ROLE PLAY THREE   A

You are a journalist. You will interview your partner, a Green politician. There is a big problem of pollution in the capital of your country. It is caused by cars.

Ask your partner:
- what he/she thinks about the problem;
- what solutions he/she proposes;
- how he/she travels.

ROLE PLAY THREE   B

You are a Green politician. There is a big problem of pollution in the capital of your country and your political party supports the banning of cars in the city centre.

You:
- think the problem is very serious;
- support the banning of all cars (except politicians' cars and ambulances);
- always travel in a big car with a motorcycle escort.

GRAMMAR NOTES: CONDITIONALS

Look at the following sentence and note its construction:

If you take these tablets, you'll sleep better.

We can also say:

You'll sleep better if you take these tablets.

And here is the 'negative' conditional.

If we don't have more nurses, the Casualty Department will close.
Unless we have more nurses, the Casualty Department will close.

Now put the verbs in the box below into the correct forms in the following sentences.

| take | cost | feel | go | prefer | be | buy | want | lose | cook |

1 If it _____ (not) too expensive, we _____ a new X-ray machine.
2 If you _____ regular exercise, you _____ better.
3 It _____ a lot of money if you _____ cosmetic surgery.
4 I _____ sausages unless you _____ vegetarian food.
5 Unless you _____ to the dentist, you _____ that tooth.

FUNCTIONS/SKILLS NOTES: DESCRIBING CAUSE AND EFFECT

When we describe cause and effect, we usually say *because*. But there are other expressions.

Cause: *Because of/Owing to/Due to* low standards of hygiene, most people died young during the nineteenth century. But now they are living longer.

Effect: *So/Consequently/Therefore* governments are spending more money on geriatric homes and hospitals.

Now put one of the cause or effect words into the sentences below.

1 In recent years many people have been injured _____ land mines.
2 Productivity improved, _____ sales went up.
3 _____ a strike, company profits fell.
4 It rained yesterday, _____ the tennis match was cancelled.
5 _____ the rock star's illness, the concert was a disaster.

Storyline

Read the following, and check that you know the words in italics.

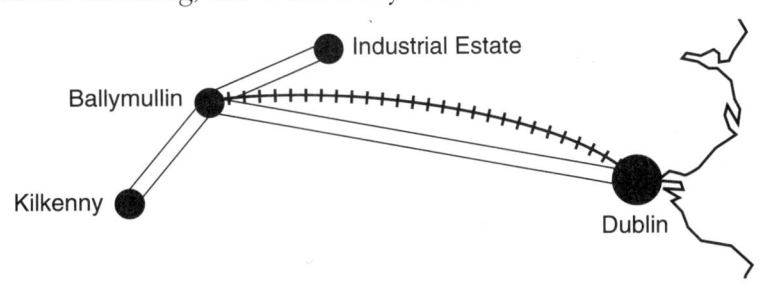

Ballymullin is a small town (20,000 inhabitants) 40 km from Dublin (Ireland). Many of its people travel to work in Dublin every day, but there is a *growing* electronics industry on the new *industrial estate* 10 km from the town. This is *attracting* young professional families to the region. Every year, about 10,000 tourists come to Ballymullin to visit its ancient *abbey*. The *mayor* of Ballymullin is Brendan Beckett, who was born there and knows the town well.

The population statistics of Ballymullin are as follows:

Category	Percentage	Trend
Retired	28%	(going down)
Working families with children	34%	(stable)
Young single people	13%	(going up)
Young professional families	12%	(going up)
Farmers and agricultural workers	13%	(going down)

64

Ballymullin has a small general hospital with a Casualty, an Obstetrics and a Paediatrics Department. It employs nine doctors and 34 nurses. Brendan Beckett is President of the Ballymullin Hospital Committee.

1 This is part of a conversation between Brendan Beckett and Moira Connolly, who works at the Irish Ministry of Health.

Read the following (mixed) questions first, then listen to the dialogue.

1. Medical standards are bad at Ballymullin Hospital.   TRUE/FALSE
2. The doctors and nurses at the hospital are (a) efficient.   (b) inefficient.
3. The hospital (a) has too many patients.   (b) does not have enough patients.
4. The hospital costs a lot of money.   TRUE/FALSE
5. The population of Ballymullin is (a) going up.   (b) going down.
6. The government will build a new hospital in Ballymullin.   TRUE/FALSE
7. The new population of Ballymullin works (a) in Dublin.
   (b) on the industrial estate.
8. The hospital in Kilkenny will be near (a) Dublin.   (b) Ballymullin.
9. There are trains to Kilkenny.   TRUE/FALSE
10. Brendan Beckett wants to close Ballymullin Hospital.   TRUE/FALSE

2 Fill in the gaps. Brendan Beckett says:

1. 'If there _____ no hospital, they _____ _____.'
2. 'If you _____ to close our hospital, there _____ trouble.'

As Brendan Beckett predicted, the people of Ballymullin were very angry when the government announced the closure of their hospital. 87% of them signed the following petition:

> We, the people of Ballymullin, protest at the closing of our hospital.
> WE:
> • demand that the hospital stays open;
> • have confidence in the medical staff;
> • will not pay taxes if the hospital closes;
> • are not afraid of prison!
> Signed

A street demonstration was planned for Saturday, 15th July.

9 Closing a Hospital   © Delta Publishing 1998

The government's plan is to:
- close Ballymullin Hospital on 31st December;
- open Kilkenny Hospital on 1 January;
- transfer medical staff to Kilkenny Hospital.

Other facts:
- The move to Kilkenny will save £2 million per year.
- The construction of Kilkenny Hospital is three months late.

Brendan Beckett was very concerned. On Wednesday, 12th July, he held a meeting. The following people were there:

1. Brendan Beckett, Chairman
2. Moira Connolly, an employee at the Ministry of Health
3. The Director of Ballymullin Hospital (an obstetrician)
4. A doctor at Ballymullin Hospital (a geriatrician)
5. The Chairperson of the Chamber of Commerce
6. The Director of Kilkenny Hospital

Role plays

ROLE ONE
You are Brendan Beckett. AGAINST closing hospital. Summarise the situation, then ask for opinions. Try to find a compromise solution.

ROLE TWO
You are Moira Connolly. FOR closing hospital. Costs too much money. Kilkenny Hospital is more modern. Perhaps government will pay for bus service to Kilkenny? (you are not sure)

ROLE THREE
You are an obstetrician and Director of Ballymullin Hospital. AGAINST closing hospital. Young population of Ballymullin going up = more babies = Obstetrics Department needed.

ROLE FOUR
You are a geriatrician at Ballymullin Hospital. UNDECIDED about closing hospital. Older population going down in Ballymullin. Transform hospital into old peoples' clinic (with you as Director)?

ROLE FIVE
You are the Chairperson of the Chamber of Commerce. AGAINST closing hospital. Young population going up. Professional families working for international companies. Need paediatric and obstetric hospital. No hospital = no company investment in industrial estate.

ROLE SIX
You are the Director of Kilkenny Hospital. FOR closing Ballymullin Hospital. Kilkenny is more modern.

Afterwards

1 Some days later, Brendan Beckett sent the following letter to Moira Connolly. Fill in the verbs (in italics) in the correct tense.

> Dear Ms Connolly,
>
> Following our meeting last Wednesday, I am writing to clarify our position.
>
> As you know, the people of Ballymullin are against closing the hospital. If the government (1) _____ (*persist*) with the idea, there (2) _____ (*be*) more demonstrations. Also, people (3) _____ (*refuse*) to pay taxes.
>
> Next, the construction of Kilkenny Hospital is three months late. If it (4) _____ (*be not finished*) until March or April, where (5) _____ you _____ (*put*) the patients?
>
> Finally, how (6) _____ the government _____ (*help*) the hospital visitors without cars? If you (7) _____ (*start*) a special hospital bus service to Kilkenny, perhaps the demonstrations (8) _____ (*stop*).
>
> I look forward to your comments.
>
> Yours sincerely,
>
> Brendan Beckett
> Brendan Beckett
> President, Ballymullin Hospital Committee

2 *How healthy are you?* You are going to interview your partner about his/her daily habits. Here are some ideas for questions:

| watching TV | drinking | night-clubs | exercise | stress at work |
| sleep | computer screens | fruit and vegetables | sport | smoking |

First, write a questionnaire based on some of the above subjects. (You can add other questions if you wish.) The following question-forms may be useful:

'Do you…?'

'How much/many … do you…?'

'How often do you…?'

Now interview your partner.

UNIT 10 — *Fireworks*

Introduction

Did you know that...?

> ...on 5th November 1605, Guy Fawkes (1570–1606) and other conspirators tried to blow up the Houses of Parliament in London. He was caught and executed. But in Britain, his exploit is celebrated every 5th November by fireworks and the burning of effigies of Guy Fawkes.

ANOTHER FIREWORKS INJURY

Linking and exchanging

But fireworks can be dangerous. In November 1996, more than 1,200 people went to hospital with injuries from fireworks and one man was killed.

1 Link the words to the pictures and write the correct letter in the space provided.

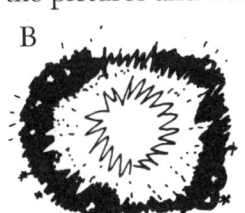

A   B   C   D

Words	Pictures
Effigies	_____
Fireworks	_____
Injuries	_____
To blow up	_____

2 Put the words in the box into the text below.

anniversary   personalities   press   speeches   party

A company's fiftieth (1) _____ is a good opportunity for publicity. Small companies usually have a (2) _____ and invite the local (3) _____. But often larger companies pay television (4) _____ to give (5) _____ or put advertisements in newspapers to celebrate their success.

| 68 |

Brayton Ltd, a well-known British software distribution company, is celebrating its tenth anniversary. Just before the dinner, the 150 employees are drinking cocktails. They are waiting for Harold Brayton, the Managing Director, to make a speech. Listen to the conversation between John and Nina, two of the employees.

3 Decide whether the sentences are true or false and circle the correct answer.

1	Nina and John have not met before.	TRUE	FALSE
2	Nina is enjoying the celebrations.	TRUE	FALSE
3	John is hungry.	TRUE	FALSE
4	John respects Harold Brayton.	TRUE	FALSE
5	Harold Brayton's speech is a success.	TRUE	FALSE
6	Nina and John leave before the end of the speech.	TRUE	FALSE

4 *General comprehension.* The dinner was not very well-organised, and the beginning of Harold Brayton's speech was not a success. What was wrong with:

1. the room temperature?
2. the bar service?
3. the microphone?
4. How can you describe the *attitude* of Harold Brayton's employees?

| friendly | hostile | generous | disrespectful | frightened |

5 *Social English.* What do Nina and John say?

1. John, *saying hello*. 'Nina! Nice _____ _____ _____. _____ _____ you?'

2. John, *offering*. '_____ _____ _____ _____ _____ drink?'

3. Nina, *accepting*. '_____. _____ whisky _____.'

4. John, *apologising*. 'But _____ _____ _____ ice, _____ _____.'

5. John, *suggesting*. '_____ _____ _____ _____ pub.'

6. Nina and John. What do they say when they drink? '_____!'

Before doing the role plays that follow, here are some more useful social English expressions:

Saying hello	(to someone you haven't met)	*Pleased to meet you.*
	(to someone you know)	*How's life?*
		How are you keeping?
Responding	(to someone you haven't met)	*Pleased to meet you.*
	(to someone you know)	*Fine, and you?*
Offering		*Would you like a …?*
Accepting		*Thank you very much.*
Refusing		*No, thank you.*
Apologising		*I'm sorry, but…*

10 Fireworks   © Delta Publishing 1998

Role plays

ROLE PLAY ONE — A

Your name: Molly/Mark Pickford

It is 11.30. You are at a conference. It is the coffee break. You see your colleague, Monika/Manfred Reich. You say hello and offer coffee.

You bring coffee, then talk.

You think: • the last speaker was boring.
You offer: • to invite him/her to lunch.

ROLE PLAY ONE — B

Your name: Monika/Manfred Reich

It is 11.30. You are at a conference. It is the coffee break. Your colleague, Molly/Mark Pickford will say hello. Accept his/her offer of coffee (with sugar).

He/she will bring the coffee, then you will talk.

You think: • the last speaker was interesting.
You accept: • his/her second offer and suggest a restaurant (use your imagination here).

ROLE PLAY TWO — A

Your name: Camilla/Carlo Battestini

It is 12.30. You are at an international conference at a hotel. It is the lunch break. From behind, you think you see your colleague, Sasha/Sergei Ulyanov. Say hello and how pleased you are to see him/her.

You apologise for your mistake, then introduce yourself and start a conversation.

You think: • it's an interesting conference;
• sound system is bad.
You hope: • food in hotel is good (you are hungry).

ROLE PLAY TWO — B

Your name: Germaine/Gérard Trevidy

It is 12.30. You are at an international conference at a hotel. It is the lunch break. Someone will say hello to you. (Note: you are not Sasha/Sergei Ulyanov.) You will have a short conversation with your partner.

You think: • it's an interesting conference;
• sound system is OK.
You know: • hotel has a bad reputation for food.

ROLE PLAY THREE — A

Your name: Susanna/Sven Angstromm

You are at a cocktail party. You meet an ex-colleague, Juanita/Juan Sanchez. You haven't seen him/her for a long time. Say hello, and offer to get him/her a drink.

Bring the drink, then talk.

You ask: • about his/her new job.
You offer: • to take him/her to dinner after the cocktail party.

ROLE PLAY THREE — B

Your name: Juanita/Juan Sanchez

You are at a cocktail party. You will meet an ex-colleague, Susanna/Sven Angstromm. You haven't seen him/her for a long time. Say hello and accept his/her offer (dry white wine).

He/she will bring your drink, then you will talk.

You tell: • him/her about your new job (Personnel Manager for the Paris office of a Spanish company).
You refuse: • his/her offer of dinner (you have a previous engagement).
You suggest: • another date and place for dinner (use your imagination here).

GRAMMAR NOTES: FUTURE TIME

There are five ways of talking about the future in English. Read the following examples:

1 **will/shall ('ll)** – the reactive future
   'I'm cold.'
   'OK. I'll close the window.'

2 **be going to do something** – plans
   'We're going to visit Greece next year.'

3 **simple present** – schedules
   'Your plane leaves at 15.45.'

4 **present continuous**
   'We're having dinner with Jim tomorrow.'

5 **shall/will ('ll) – continuous**
   'I'll be staying at the Sea View Hotel.'

Often there is little difference between the use of these tenses, but they are not always interchangeable.

FORECASTING

When we talk or write about the future, we are often *unsure* about what we say. So we make *forecasts*, with different predictions of certainty. Here are some of the words/expressions we use:

100% certainty – I am *sure/certain* that we must export…
75% sure   – Brayton *should/will probably* get the contract.
50% sure   – he *may/might* be late tomorrow, there's a rail strike.
25% sure   – It's *unlikely* she'll come to the meeting.

Storyline

Nightspark is a British company situated in Bratwich in the north of England, a region of high unemployment. It has manufactured fireworks for over a hundred years, and employs 65 (mainly unqualified) people. Until now, Nightspark has sold mainly in the domestic market, so its exports are low.

The number of accidents caused by fireworks has increased recently, so the British government has restricted the sale of fireworks. The future for Nightspark is not good.

1 *Reading comprehension.* Answer the following:

   1 If Nightspark closes, it will be bad for the employees. Why?

   2 It will not be easy for Nightspark to export more. Why not?

   3 The sale of fireworks has been restricted. Why?

   4 Nightspark's future is not good. Why not?

Now read the following story from a popular London newspaper.

TV PERSONALITY INJURED

Lottie Bruce, the well-known TV actress, is in hospital with shock. She was the guest of honour at the tenth anniversary of Brayton Ltd. Just after the dinner, she started the fireworks. But they all exploded together. One of the witnesses said it was 'like a bomb'. Seven Brayton employees are in hospital with burns.

Harold Brayton, the Managing Director, said, 'I am extremely sorry about Lottie Bruce and very angry. Our anniversary was ruined!' We have not been able to contact Nightspark, the manufacturer of the fireworks.

2 *Reading comprehension*. Answer the following.

1 How many people are in hospital? _____

2 Why was Lottie Bruce at the anniversary? _____

3 What happened to the fireworks? _____

4 Harold Brayton is (a) sorry about his employees.
               (b) angry about the anniversary.

5 The newspaper (a) has spoken to a representative from Nightspark.
               (b) has not spoken to a representative from Nightspark.

3 You will listen to a meeting between four members of the Nightspark management. They are:

    Jack Napp   – Managing Director
    Christine Bridges – Personnel Manager
    Javesh Patel   – Security Manager
    Trish Jameson   – Public Relations Manager

Now answer the following mixed comprehension questions about the current situation.

1 Javesh Patel wants Trish Jameson to make a press statement saying that
_____

2 Trish Jameson (a) agrees with the idea.
               (b) is not happy with the idea.

3 Javesh Patel thinks Lottie Bruce will benefit from the _____

4 Jack Napp is (a) concerned about Lottie Bruce.
              (b) not concerned about Lottie Bruce.

5 He thinks Harold Brayton will ask for _____

6 Seven of Harold Brayton's employees are seriously ill.   TRUE/FALSE

4 *Action plans*. Jack Napp gives various orders.

   1 He will _____

   2 Trish Jameson will _____

   3 Javesh Patel will _____

   4 Christine Bridges will _____

5 *Forecasting*. Fill in the missing words.

   1 'Look, I'm _____ _____ she won't start…'

   2 '…Brayton. _____ _____ ask for damages.'

   3 '…site. You _____ find Brayton's didn't follow the …'

   4 'It's _____.'

   5 '…in cash. They _____ accept that.'

Three days after the meeting

Nightspark's immediate problems have been solved:
- Lottie Bruce had good publicity and didn't start a scandal.
- Jack Napp agreed on a private financial arrangement with Harold Brayton.
- Harold Brayton's company did not follow all the safety rules.
- The people in hospital accepted the cash payments.

But Jack Napp is still concerned about the future of Nightspark.
The situation is this:
- Fireworks can be dangerous.
- Domestic sales are falling.
- UK government restrictions on firework sales are increasing.
- There was bad newspaper publicity about the Brayton incident.

But, more positively:
- There are markets for fireworks in other countries (especially South America and Central Europe) with fewer government restrictions.
- Nightspark can perhaps manufacture other paper products (decorations etc.) or recycle used paper to make stationery.

Jack Napp decides to have a third meeting with the management of Nightspark to discuss the situation.

Role play – The future of Nightspark

The aim of this meeting is to decide on future company policy. There are six people present:

Jack Napp – Managing Director
Christine Bridges – Personnel Manager
Javesh Patel – Security Manager
Trish Jameson – Public Relations Manager
Winston Tooley – Production Manager
Janet Duggan – Sales Manager

ROLE ONE

You are Jack Napp, Chairperson of the meeting. Begin by summarising the situation and describing the alternatives. Then ask for opinions.
You are *undecided* about what to do.
Your main concern is that Nightspark continues in business.

ROLE TWO

You are Christine Bridges.
You:
- have two small children and are concerned about safety;
- want Nightspark to abandon fireworks and make other products;
- do not want more unemployment in Bratwitch;
- are against exporting fireworks because they are dangerous.

ROLE THREE

You are Javesh Patel. You have worked at Nightspark for only six months.
You want:
- to close the factory in Bratwitch;
- to open one in Central Europe.

You speak good German and some Russian, so you would be the ideal manager for a Central European factory.

ROLE FOUR

You are Trish Jameson. You are concerned about the recent bad publicity, but also about unemployment in Bratwitch.
You:
- want Nightspark to make safer fireworks;
- are in favour of paper recycling to make stationery (good for the public image of Nightspark).

ROLE FIVE

You are Winston Tooley. You have worked at Nightspark all your life. Your son and two daughters work at Nightspark also. You think the safety problems are exaggerated by the press.
You want:
- to continue manufacturing fireworks in Bratwitch;
- to develop sales to Central Europe and South America.

If Nightspark closes its factory, you and your family will be unemployed.

ROLE SIX

You are Janet Duggan. You have worked at Nightspark for two years.
You:
- are concerned about government restrictions and falling sales;
- want to close the factory in Bratwitch and open one in South America (cheaper cost of labour).

Your brother is an import agent in South America. Perhaps he can represent Nightspark's interests.

Afterwards

1 You are Jack Napp. Following the decision of the meeting, write an open letter to the employees of Nightspark. Basically, there were three possibilities:
- to continue manufacturing fireworks in Bratwitch;
- to start manufacturing some other product;
- to relocate production to another country.

Give the *reasons* for the decision, the *advantages* for the company and the *consequences* for the employees. And try to be positive about the future.

Examples: 'We *are sure* that sales will rise…'
'Exports *should improve* our sales.' (etc.)

Following the incident at Brayton Ltd last month, the management of Nightspark has made some important decisions.

First of all, _____

_____

_____

_____

_____

_____

_____

---

2 You live near London (UK). You met your Senegalese colleague, Corinne Sylla, at a conference in Dakar (Senegal) last year. You have just received a fax from her. She will come to London next month for an English language training course. You send her the following fax in reply. Circle the correct words from the choice given in *italics*:

FAX

Dear (1) *Corinne/Corinne Sylla/Sylla*,

I'm very (2) *pleasing/pleased/pleasure* to hear from you again. I hope you are (3) *good/fine/well*. Please (4) *to tell me/say me/let me know* when you arrive and I'll come (5) *to/from/at* the airport to meet you.

If you (6) *will have/have/would have* any free time in London, I'll take you to some art galleries and museums. As you know, (7) *I'm living/I lived/I live* in a small town near London, and I hope that you will stay at my house during the weekends.

I look forward to (8) *see/seeing/saw* you again.

Best wishes,

_____ (your name)

ROLE PLAY FORM

YOUR NAME: _____

YOUR ROLE: _____

Main points: _____

_____

_____

_____

You want: _____

_____

_____

ROLE PLAY FORM

YOUR NAME: _____

YOUR ROLE: _____

Main points: _____

_____

_____

_____

You want: _____

_____

_____

ROLE PLAY FORM

YOUR NAME: _____

YOUR ROLE: _____

Main points: _____

_____

_____

_____

You want: _____

_____

_____

© Delta Publishing 1998
This page may be photocopied under the terms outlined on p.ii.

TAPESCRIPT

Unit 1

CONVERSATION 1

Receptionist (R)
Client (C)

R: Schiller Hotel, good afternoon.
C: Good afternoon. I'd like to book a room, please.
R: Certainly, madam. When for, please?
C: From the 5th to the 7th of July.
R: Just a minute please, I'll have a look…. What sort of room?
C: A single, with a bath preferably.
R: I'm afraid we only have showers.
C: Oh, that'll be alright.
R: The 5th to the 7th. Yes, that's OK.
C: Does the room have a television?
R: Oh, yes. There's a TV and mini-bar in every room.
C: Good.
R: Could you give me your name, please?
C: Wales, Jennifer Wales. That's W-A-L-E-S.
R: Right, Mrs Wiles, I've got that.
C: No, not Wiles. Wales. With an A. And it's Ms, not Mrs.
R: Sorry. I've got it now, Ms Wales.
C: How much is the room, please?
R: 220 deutschmarks per night, with breakfast at 27,50.
C: And is service included?
R: Yes, it is. How would you like to pay, Ms Wales?
C: Credit card, if that's OK.
R: Certainly. May I have the number?
C: It's… wait a moment… ah, yes 5231 8576 6960 9702.
R: Right. So that's a single room with shower for two nights from the 5th to the 7th of July in the name of Ms Jennifer Wales. The room price is 220 deutschmarks and your credit card number is 5231 8576 6960 9702. Can you confirm this by fax, please?
C: OK. What's your fax number?
R: 49 351 20 654 76.
C: Right, I've got that. I'll send the fax today.
R: Thank you very much. Goodbye, Ms Wales.
C: Goodbye.

CONVERSATION 2

John Swift (JS)
Senora Catalla (SC)

SC: Good afternoon.
JS: Good afternoon, madam. Can I help you?
SC: I telephoned you last week to reserve a room for tonight. The name's Catalla.
JS: Right… er… Catalla, you said?
SC: That's it.
JS: C-A…
SC: …T-A-double L-A.
JS: I can't seem to… ah yes, here we are. But you're booked in for *tomorrow* night, Mrs Catalla.
SC: But I confirmed the booking by fax.
JS: Did you? Well, I can't find it.
SC: I see. Do you have a room? A single, with shower.
JS: I'm afraid there are no singles left for tonight. But we do have a suite.
SC: And how much is that?
JS: 725 deutschmarks.
SC: That's much too expensive.
JS: Well, why don't you try the Harbour Hotel. It's just across the street.
SC: There's no alternative, is there? I only hope the Harbour Hotel is more efficient than you, Mr Swift.
JS: Goodbye, Mrs Catalla. Oh, God…

Unit 2

PRESENTATION 1

Good morning, ladies and gentlemen, and welcome to Bailey Instruments. My name is Jennie Knight. In a few minutes we'll go into the meeting room and I'll tell you about the company. Following that, my colleague, Jeremy Stevens is going to show you round the Production department, then Myriam Snowden will present our R&D department. And after that we'll have lunch together in Bailey's staff restaurant, which is very good. But first, let's have coffee. By the way, if you want to wash your hands, the toilets are over there to the left. Are there any questions?

PRESENTATION 2

Paco Cordobes (PC)
Q = Questioner

PC: Good afternoon, ladies and gentlemen. My name's Paco Cordobes, and I'm the Personnel Manager of Vestimenta del Mar. As you know, we manufacture waterproof clothing for seamen. First, I'll tell you about the company and its products, then we'll look at the future developments.

Vestimenta del Mar was founded in 1952. At the beginning it was a small family company with local outlets to the fishing industry here in Vigo. The situation changed during the eighties, and especially after 1986, when Spain joined the European Union.

As you can see from this slide, our activities have expanded. We have two regional warehouses, one down here in Barcelona, the other there, near Malaga in the south of Spain. And we export nearly 14 per cent of our production, mainly to other European countries.

Right, let's turn to personnel. Vestimenta del Mar employs about 70 people, mostly here in Vigo, where there are around 50 production staff and 12 managerial and administrative personnel. Also, as you can see, we employ five sales people at the warehouses – two in Malaga and three in Barcelona. Now we'll have a look at our products and… We can see from this table that our largest market is in clothing for seamen, with 62 per cent of total domestic sales. But there is also a growing market

in the Mediterranean for light waterproof clothing for leisure sailing. This represents only 24 per cent of our sales at present, but it is growing.
Q: What percentage of the light clothing do you sell in France?
PC: Well, not very much, in fact. You see, French seamen prefer to buy…
Q: … French clothing.
PC: Well, yes.
Q: It's normal, no?
PC: Er, I suppose so. Now, let's turn to the future of…

Unit 3

Conversation 1

Andrea Matthews (AM)
Lufthansa Receptionist (LR)

LR: Can I help you, madam?
AM: Er… I'm booked on a flight to Berlin and I'm not sure which gate number.
LR: May I see your ticket, please?
AM: Here it is.
LR: Thank you. Yes, the Lufthansa flight 4501 to Berlin. Ah, I'm sorry, but take-off has been delayed.
AM: Oh, no. How long will I have to wait?
LR: About an hour, I'm afraid.
AM: Oh, hell. That means I'll be late for an appointment.
LR: I see. Look, I'll try and book you onto another flight.
AM: OK. Thanks very much.
LR: Would you take a seat?

Conversation 2

Andrea Matthews (AM)
Angela Davies (AD)

AD: Research Department, can I help you?
AM: Angela? Hello, it's Andrea.
AD: Hello, Andrea. Everything OK in Berlin?
AM: Yes, fine. But… er… there's a problem.
AD: Oh yeah.
AM: You see, I've arranged to stay an extra night here, till the 8th. But the thing is, I've got an appointment with Dr Kalowska in Warsaw at 2 p.m. on the 7th. And that's tomorrow.
AD: Hm-hm.
AM: So, could you ring him tomorrow morning and change it to the afternoon of the 9th?
AD: But why don't you…
AM: I tried ringing him, but there's no reply.
AD: OK, Andrea. I'll arrange it and send you a fax. But it'll cost you a bottle of vodka.
AM: Thanks so much, Angela.
AD: Oh, that's OK.
AM: And I won't forget the vodka. Promise. Bye.
AD: Bye, Andrea. Every trip there's a problem.

Unit 4

Conversation 1

Manager: Good evening, madam.
Customer: Good evening. I've reserved a table for three.
Manager: And the name?
Customer: Hoskins.
Manager: Oh yes, if you'll follow me. Here we are.
Customer: But it's right beside the toilets. That's no good.

Conversation 2

Waiter: Are you ready to order, sir?
Customer: Ready? We've been waiting for half an hour.
Waiter: I'm sorry, sir. But it's Saturday night, you see.
Customer: Why don't you get more staff?
Waiter: Well, we've only just opened and…

Conversation 3

Waitress: Here's your bill, sir.
Man: Thank you. Now where's my cheque book?
Waitress: I'm afraid we don't accept cheques, sir.
Man: What? You don't accept cheques? What the hell…
Woman: Oh, stop it, Charlie. I'll pay by credit card.
Waitress: Thank you, madam.

Conversation 4

Jerry Stacks (JS)
Anna Waleska (AW)

JS: Look, something's wrong, Anna. We've invested over a million dollars in Poland, but every night our restaurants are almost empty.
AW: Yes, I know. But it's very competitive here. Do you know how many fast food restaurants there are in Poland? Nearly three hundred. And…
JS: But Pizza World is *not* fast food. It's quality Italian cuisine.
AW: Yes, and that's the second problem.
JS: What do you mean?
AW: It's a question of image. People *think* that Pizza World is just another American food company.
JS: Hm. So what do you suggest?
AW: Basically, a change of image.
JS: You mean selling hamburgers?
AW: No, Jerry, not hamburgers. But a pizza home delivery service, that's what we need. But it'll mean investment – delivery personnel, scooters, that sort of thing. And a new advertising campaign to attract younger people.
JS: So you want Pizza World to compete with the hamburger bars?
AW: No. I want Pizza World to invest in a home delivery service. It's simple really, and it won't cost much.
JS: How much?
AW: Well – fifteen scooters …. Say about two hundred and fifty thousand zlotys.
JS: Two hundred and fifty thousand. I'll see what I can do, Anna, but it's going to be…

Unit 5

Conversation 1

Sports journalist (SJ)
Tommy Moore (TM)

SJ: Bad defeat today, Tommy, wasn't it?
TM: It was a disappointment, yes.
SJ: Your fifth defeat in a row.
TM: Yes.
SJ: And there weren't many supporters, were there?

TM: That's true.
SJ: So how can Barnfield continue? I mean, without supporters a team loses money and…
TM: I know that. But first we must find good players, players who score goals. Then the supporters will come back. And then we'll make money again.
SJ: So what do you plan to do?
TM: Get a new trainer. New players from abroad. And you'll see, next year we'll be back in the Second Division.
SJ: But how will you pay…
TM: I've got no more comments.
SJ: Thank you, Tomm– Mr Moore.

CONVERSATION 2

Tommy Moore (TM)
Wim Nugteren (WN)

TM: Come in, Wim. Sit down.
WN: Thanks.
TM: I've just received this letter. Have a look.
WN: Only 350 thousand for our best player! That's ridiculous.
TM: If Junio's our best player, tell me why he's only scored five goals this season.
WN: Well, it's the climate. He doesn't like the cold weather. But he's popular with the supporters.
TM: Wim, supporters have fallen by 15 per cent this season. We're still in the Third Division. If we don't win more matches, Totley Holdings will stop sponsorship. And you're making excuses for a player who doesn't like the cold weather?
WN: OK, we're still in the Third Division. But whose fault is that? Not Junio's.
TM: No, Wim. It's yours. You're the man who's responsible for team discipline. You must be more strict.
WN: But how? The players are my friends.
TM: You're their trainer, not their friend. And here's how – extra training sessions before each match. And if players miss them, you cut their salaries by £25 each time. And no more night-clubs.
WN: There'll be a revolution.
TM: Your problem, Wim.
WN: And Junio? If he goes to Italy, we'll lose even more supporters.
TM: That's my problem.

Unit 6

CONVERSATION 1

Danny: Not many people today, are there?
Mike: That's only 'cause the food's bad.
Danny: Oh? My sausages are alright. How're yours, Mike?
Mike: Terrible – as usual. Anyway, this place is going to be closed soon.
Danny: Closed?
Mike: Well, that's what I heard. They're going to install vending machines.
Danny: But why?
Mike: Nobody uses the canteen.
Danny: But this is the only place we can talk and relax. And they always break down, vending machines.
Mike: I think it's a good idea. It'll save time and space. Be more efficient as well
Danny: Huh, you talk like the bosses.
Mike: No, it's just that…

CONVERSATION 2

Antonio da Costa (AC)
Lars Petersson (LP)
Maria Silva (MS)

AC: Well, let's start. As you can see, the plan is to put the food and coffee vending machines just there – beside the offices. This will give us 250 square metres more production area. First, we will transform the present entry hall and put the toilets there, where the kitchens are now. Then we'll make the canteen entry into a visitors' entry – there, between the toilets and the first-aid post. Also, we'll put a visitors' car park opposite the new entry. A big advantage is that the office staff will be next to the vending machines, so coffee breaks will be shorter.
MS: But they won't be very near the toilets, will they?
AC: Er, well. That's true, yes. But the main problem is the cost – over a hundred thousand dollars.
LP: Yes, it's very expensive.
MS: And that's not the only problem, Antonio. What about the staff? How will they react? They've always had a canteen where they can relax during breaks.
LP: Well, you must explain that –
MS: But this won't be popular, Lars. I can tell you.
AC: Well, what about a…

Unit 7

CONVERSATION 1

Mary Flanagan (MF)
Adam Bales (AB)

AB: Well, Mary, how are things?
MF: Not too good. Look, I've brought this graph. My profits from '92 onwards.
AB: Right, let's have a look. Erm… profits good in '92… and rising in '93… and you had a peak in '94.
MF: Yes, but look at '95, Adam. They started to fall.
AB: Yes, from 15 to 12 thousand pounds. But they went up again in '96.
MF: That was only because of that fire in the supermarket. They closed for two months, remember?
AB: Oh, yes. Penrose was furious.
MF: Yes, wasn't he? But then they re-opened. And look at my profits in '97. Down by three thousand.
AB: And now?
MF: They're still falling. Look at the graph. What can I do, Adam?
AB: Well, what about…?

CONVERSATION 2

Sharon Mitchell (SM)
Lenny Graft (LG)

LG: Good morning everybody, and welcome to Hampshire Business News. Today I'm going to talk to Sharon Mitchell. Sharon is a partner in Market Organics, a local organic food producer. Good morning, Sharon.

SM:	Good morning, Lenny.
LG:	Now, Sharon. Market Organics has been very successful, hasn't it? I mean, you sell your products in all the high-class food shops.
SM:	That's true. It wasn't easy at first, but –
LG:	But you want to expand into supermarkets. Why is that?
SM:	Well, two reasons. First, the market in food shops is almost saturated. And then, obviously, we want to expand our business.
LG:	But aren't you too expensive for supermarkets?
SM:	No, I don't think so at all. You see, Lenny, these days people are buying quality food. They don't want industrial –
LG:	But will they pay your prices?
SM:	They'll pay for quality, Lenny.
LG:	Yes, OK. But Market Organics is small, isn't it?
SM:	We have 34 employees.
LG:	But what about advertising? I mean, it's expensive. How will you reach the supermarket customer?
SM:	Well… on local radio and in the newspapers at first. Then on television.
LG:	Television?
SM:	Not immediately of course, but –
LG:	Sharon, aren't you being too ambitious?
SM:	Too ambitious? Of course not.
LG:	Well, I hope you succeed. Thank you for coming onto Hampshire Business News. And tomorrow we will hear from a…

Unit 8

Conversation 1

A = department store assistant
B = woman customer

A:	Good morning, madam.
B:	Good morning. Look, I'm afraid I've got a complaint.
A:	Yes, madam?
B:	Look at this dress. I bought it three weeks ago.
A:	Yes?
B:	Well, see here. The colours are all faded… and I only washed it once.
A:	Yes, I see. Do you have a receipt, madam?
B:	Of course. Here you are.
A:	Thank you. I'll replace it immediately.
B:	No, that's no good. I want a refund.

Conversation 2

Oliver Jakhri (OJ)
Françoise Bernardon (FB)

FB:	Good afternoon, Mr Jakhri.
OJ:	Hello, Françoise. How are you?
FB:	Quite well, thank you. Please sit down.
OJ:	Thank you.
FB:	Mr Jakhri, I'll speak frankly. We've had a lot of complaints about your dresses.
OJ:	Complaints? What do you mean?
FB:	The colours fade after washing.
OJ:	But that's not possible, they –
FB:	It's true, Mr Jakhri. We tested them.
OJ:	I see.
FB:	And that's not all. Your last delivery was three weeks late.
OJ:	But there were strikes, and –
FB:	That's not my problem.
OJ:	Françoise, we've supplied Bonprix for over fifteen years. We know what you want.
FB:	What we want, Mr Jakhri, is better quality, more efficient delivery and lower prices.
OJ:	Lower prices?
FB:	Fifteen per cent lower.
OJ:	Fifteen per cent? That's impossible!
FB:	There are other suppliers, Mr Jakhri.

Unit 9

Conversation 1

Interviewer (I)
Jackie Palmer (JP)

I:	Ms Palmer, in your opinion, what's the main problem with our health services today?
JP:	Basically, age. You see, people are living longer. And if a man retires at 60, he can live for another 25 years. But he'll need health services near his home.
I:	But why is that so difficult?
JP:	Because the government's closing a lot of small hospitals to save money.
I:	And you think this is dangerous for older people?
JP:	Yes, I do. Especially if the nearest hospital's 80 kilometres away. The government's concentrating too much on…

Conversation 2

Moira Connolly (MC)
Brendan Beckett (BB)

MC:	You see, Mr Beckett, the hospital costs too much and it's not working efficiently.
BB:	But our standards of medicine are very high.
MC:	Of course they are. It's not the medical standards. But half the beds are usually empty. That's the problem.
BB:	Look, the population of Ballymullin's going up every day. New people are coming to work on the industrial estate. Professional families with children. If there's no hospital, they won't come. Not with children.
MC:	Mr Beckett, the hospital's old.
BB:	Yes, I know but –
MC:	And we're building a new one, near Dublin, only 30 kilometres from here.
BB:	Where?
MC:	In Kilkenny.
BB:	But there's no rail link to Kilkenny. How will families visit the hospital?
MC:	There's a road.
BB:	What about people without cars? I'm sorry, Ms Connolly, but your plan won't work. If you try to close our hospital, there'll be trouble. And that's for sure.

Unit 10

Conversation 1

John (J)
Nina (N)
Harold Brayton (HB)

- **N:** Hello, John.
- **J:** Nina! Nice to see you. How are you?
- **N:** To be frank, hungry and cold.
- **J:** So am I. Why don't they turn on the heating?
- **N:** Electricity's expensive, you know.
- **J:** Can I get you a drink?
- **N:** Thanks. A whisky, please.
- **J:** Here we are, but there's no more ice, I'm afraid. Cheers.
- **N:** Cheers.
- **J:** Hope old Brayton's speech isn't long.
- **N:** Shush. He's starting now.
- **HB:** Ladies and gentlemen, I have great pleasure in… oh hell…
- **N:** Well, that was a short speech.
- **HB:** Ah yes… in welcoming you to the tenth anniversary celebrations of our company. As you know… we at Brayton have always been proud of our products and … so I am especially happy this evening to…
- **J:** Bla… bla… . Let's go to the pub. It's warm there.
- **N:** Right!

Conversation 2

Jack Napp (JN)
Christine Bridges (CB)
Javesh Patel (JP)
Trish Jameson (TJ)

- **JN:** Well, what do we do?
- **JP:** Trish must make a statement to the press.
- **TJ:** Saying what?
- **JP:** That our fireworks are safe.
- **TJ:** Safe? With Lottie Bruce in hospital?
- **JP:** It's good publicity for her. Name in the papers.
- **TJ:** But –
- **JN:** Look, I'm fairly sure she won't start a scandal. I'm more concerned about Harold Brayton. He'll probably ask for damages.
- **CB:** And remember, seven of his people are in hospital.
- **JN:** How are they, by the way?
- **CB:** Nothing serious.
- **JN:** Thank God for that. Look, I'll contact Harold Brayton and try to agree on a private arrangement. But the situation's serious. We must act fast. Trish, make a statement to the press saying that we regret the incident and hope Lottie Bruce will leave hospital soon.
- **TJ:** And the seven employees?
- **JN:** Oh, them as well, of course. And Javesh, go and inspect the site. You may find Brayton's didn't follow the safety rules.
- **JP:** It's unlikely.
- **JN:** And Christine, go and see the people in hospital and offer them say, £500… no, £300 in cash. They should accept that.
- **CB:** OK.
- **JN:** Right, that's that for today. Thank you, everybody. And we'll meet again in three days to review progress. That's Friday at 10. OK?
- **ALL:** Alright. OK.

Teacher's Notes and Answer Keys

Unit 1

Part One

Pre-teach: *creche   to welcome   tip   vegetarian*

The aim of the Introduction and Linking and exchanging activities is to help learners use the language of hotels with confidence.

Exercises 1 to 4 can be done individually or in pairs. The Grammar Notes are optional, though the Skills Notes should be done as they will be needed later.

Exercise 5. Play the cassette as often as necessary, homing in on the formulae of requests etc.

The role plays are designed as back-to-back telephone conversations. Check telephone formulae and the accuracy of the numerical information. Also, how well did the learners negotiate the minor problems (e.g. colour TV, but not satellite)?

Part Two

Pre-teach: *suite   to complain   to dismiss*

John Swift is obviously inefficient, and the Hayes Hotel in Hamburg has problems. Point this up.

These are pair role plays (with Role Play Four in two phases). Thorough preparation is essential to their success, so make sure each learner understands the situation and has some idea of how he/she can respond before the role play starts.

Discussion. This is optional, and depends on group level.

Afterwards. Exercise 1 is for higher-level groups while Exercise 2 is simply a review of basic vocabulary.

Unit 1 Key

Part One

Linking and exchanging

1. | Business hotels | Holiday hotels | Both |
    |---|---|---|
    | Fax machines | Night-club | Swimming pool |
    | Secretarial service | Crèche | Restaurant |
    | Foreign exchange | | TV |
    | Conference rooms | | Laundry service |
    | | | Bar |
    | | | Room service |

2. The manager – in an office
    The bar staff – behind the bar
    The chef – in the kitchen
    The waiters and waitresses – in the restaurant
    The receptionist – at the reception desk

3. The receptionist welcomes guests.
    The manager manages the hotel.
    The bar staff pour drinks.
    The waiters and waitresses serve at tables.
    The chef prepares the menus.

4. A washbasin
    B shower
    C double bed
    D toilet
    E single bed

Grammar notes

Quantity		Frequency	
100%	all	1	Always
85%	most	2	Usually
70%	many/much	3	Often
40%	some	4	Sometimes
20%	little/few	5	Never
0%	none/no		

5. The hotel receptionist noted:
    Family name: Wales
    First name: Jennifer
    Arrival date: 5 July
    Departure date: 7 July
    Accommodation: Single, with shower
    Room number: 13
    Payment: Card 5231 8576 6960 9702
    Confirmation: by fax
    The client noted:
    Price of room: DM 220
    Price of breakfast: DM 27,50
    Fax number: 49 351 20 654 76

6. 1 I'd like to
    2 Certainly
    3 I'm afraid
    4 Could
    5 Can

Part Two

Storyline

1. 1 True
    2 False
    3 False
    4 True
    5 True

2. Name: Catalla
    Price: 725 deutschmarks
    Alternative hotel: Harbour Hotel

3. 1 It was booked for the wrong date.
    2 It was too expensive.
    3 She went to another hotel.

Afterwards

1. – Directors'
    – number of
    – concerned
    – affect
    – take

2. Family name: Blackwell
    First name: George
    Arrival date: 7 April
    Departure date: 9 April
    Telephone: 0131 869 9583
    Arrival time: approx 6 p.m.
    Type of room: Single + shower
    Price: £65/night
    Room number: 215
    Payment: credit card

Unit 2

Part One

Pre-teach: *to mention   to be delayed   fog   to be founded   industrial estate   warehouse   turnover   to expand   to stock   to lay off*

The Introduction and Exercise 1 are designed to help learners with the formulae used for greetings etc. Pay attention to intonation. If you teach in-service learners, ask the questions in the Introduction, they may help indirectly with the role plays later on.

Exercises 2 and 3, the cassette presentation. Play the cassette as often as necessary.

Exercise 4. A typical social conversation followed by an optional mini-simulation.

Exercise 5. The aim here is to introduce the lexis and verbs associated with presenting companies.

The Grammar Notes and Skills Notes are optional, but could provide useful reinforcement.

Part Two

Pre-teach: *fibreglass   (car) bodies   seasonal*

This storyline is about Vestimenta del Mar, a Spanish company that manufactures clothes for seamen.

Exercise 1. These words are used in the presentation in Exercise 2, so should be checked beforehand.

Exercises 2 to 4 cover the same presentation, and the cassette will need to be played several times.

Role Plays. These are designed as group activities, but could work for pairs also. Allow time for learners to assimilate the introductory 'Presenter' and 'Visitors' information-boxes. Check that all is clear before the role plays begin. After the role plays, give feedback on their communicative success or otherwise as well as just correcting language errors.

Afterwards. Exercise 1 is open-ended and involves writing a letter of thanks, while Exercise 2 is a review of verbs.

Unit 2 Key

Part One

Linking and exchanging

1 A mixed group at 8.00 a.m. – Good morning, ladies and gentlemen.
A group of women at 3.00 p.m. – Good afternoon, ladies.
A group of men at 9.00 a.m. – Good morning, gentlemen.
Colleagues at 10.00 a.m. – Morning, everybody.
Colleagues at any time – Hello, everybody.

2
1 D
2 B
3 E
4 A
5 C

3
1 In a few minutes
2 Following that
3 then
4 After that
5 first

4 – Would you like a coffee?
– Did you have a good trip?
– Oh? What happened?
– What's your hotel like?
– And did you find Bailey easily?

5
a 8
b 6
c 5
d 1
e 4
f 9
g 2
h 10
i 7
j 3

Grammar notes
Prepositions of time
1 in
2 on, at
3 in
4 at, on
5 in

Part Two

Storyline

1 waterproof – water-resistant
seamen – professional sailors
local outlets – local markets
leisure sailing – holiday sailing

2
1 Personnel
2 seamen
3 1952
4 1986
5 Barcelona, Malaga
6 nearly 14%
7 70
8 around 50, 12
9 62
10 24

3
1 I'll tell you about
2 we'll look at
3 you can see from this
4 let's turn to
5 we'll have a look at

4
1 a
2 a
3 b
4 b

Afterwards

1 Open-ended
2 export – import
expand – contract
lose – gain
fall – rise
start – stop

1 gain
2 rose
3 imports
4 expanded
5 stopped

Unit 3

Part One

Pre-teach: *to be delayed   to oversleep*

Part One of this unit looks at the problems involved in business travel, while Part Two concretises this theme by portraying the relations between a not-very-organised business traveller and her assistant.

The Introduction and the Linking and exchanging activities (Exercises 1 and 2) are designed to introduce key words of business travel.

Exercise 3 introduces certain words necessary for this unit.

Exercises 4 and 5. Play the cassette as often as necessary, homing in on the formulae of offers and requests.

Role Plays One to Three. These are designed for pairwork and have limited aims – stating problems and offering information/suggestions.

The Grammar Notes are for information and the Functions/Skills Notes for possible use in the role plays.

PART TWO

Pre-teach: *to solve   furniture*

The first part of the storyline deals with Andrea Matthews's business trip to Germany and Poland.

Role Plays Four to Six demand rigorous class management. They are designed for mini-groups of three learners, and their order is as follows:

   Role Play Four: A1 – B1 – B2 – C – B3 – A2 – B4
   Role Play Five: A – B1 – C1 – C2 – B2 – B3
   Role Play Six: A1 – B1 – C – B2 – A2

However, the role plays can be simplified somewhat by dispensing with B (Sonja/Sven Alborg) and having the various Sales Managers of Aardvark Furniture contact C (Salma/Samir Bekkali) directly. This would involve making certain changes to the role cards. After the role plays, give feedback on telephone language as well as errors.

Afterwards. Exercise 1 is for more advanced groups, while Exercise 2 reviews the lexis of business travel.

Unit 3 Key

PART ONE

Linking and exchanging

1   A gate   F passport control
    B arrivals   G boarding
    C departures   H waiting
    D exchange   I first
    E check-in   J cabin

2   The flight was delayed so he was late for the meeting **or** so they went by Eurostar.

   The Hayes Hotel was fully booked so they stayed in another one.

   Flights to Brussels were cancelled so they went by Eurostar **or** so he was late for the meeting.

   The train left on time but she overslept.

   She arrived at 9.00 a.m. but the meeting was at 4.00 p.m.

3   research – investigation
    based – situated
    attends – goes to
    trips – journeys
    arranges – organises
    bookings – reservations

4   1 The gate number.
    2 Take-off was delayed.
    3 She will miss an appointment.
    4 Book Andrea Matthews on another flight.

5   1 Can I help you
    2 May I see your
    3 I'm sorry
    4 I'm afraid

    5 That means
    6 Would you take

PART TWO

Storyline

1   1 False
    2 False
    3 True
    4 True
    5 False
    6 False
    7 True

2   1 She wants to stay an extra night in Berlin.
    2 The 7th at 2.00 p.m.
    3 The afternoon of the 9th.
    4 Yes. There was no reply.
    5 To arrange a new appointment and send Andrea Matthews a fax.
    6 A bottle of vodka.

3   1 But the thing is
    2 could you ring him
    3 don't you
    4 I'll arrange

Afterwards

    1 wrong   6   arranged
    2 overslept   7   attend
    3 missed   8   organised
    4 broke down   9   on time
    5 booking   10 couldn't

Unit 4

PART ONE

Pre-teach: *service   fresh   to share   mineral water*

Part One of this unit covers a lot of the language used in restaurants and Part Two looks at the problems encountered in Poland by a US chain of pizza restaurants.

Introduction and Linking and exchanging (Exercises 1 to 4). These activities highlight various aspects of restaurant eating (problems – Exercise 1, current language – Exercise 2, and a spelling activity – Exercise 3).

The rest of Part One follows the fortunes of the Oasis Restaurant in the UK.

Exercise 4. Play each of the three conversations separately. All deal with relatively minor problems at the Oasis Restaurant. Go for global comprehension before asking learners to do the exercises.

Role Plays One to Three. These pair role plays propose fairly typical conflicts in day-to-day restaurant management. Note that Role Play One has three participants.

The Grammar Notes are optional, but the Functions/Skills exercise should be done as it provides reinforcement of the work of Exercise 2.

PART TWO

Pre-teach: *ambitious*

The main dilemma of Pizza World in Poland is that the public confuses it with US fast food restaurants – a question of image. This leads to disappointing results and a conflict between the US management and the local manager, who leaves the company. The story continues with the search for a replacement and interview and presentation activities.

Exercises 1 to 4. Play the cassette as often as necessary, doing each exercise in turn. Check that the concept of a pizza home delivery service is understood.

After the learners have read and understood Jerry Stack's fax to Anna Waleska, you could ask what they would do in her place... which would lead on to her resignation and the job advertisement.

Exercise 5 is basic job-searching vocabulary.
The curriculum vitae and interviews are designed as pair role plays. First, divide the class evenly into Interviewers and Candidates. Give the Interviewers the 'information-boxes', making sure that they understand they have lost the candidates' CVs. Then give the Candidates their 'information-boxes' along with their 'Candidatures' (shared out equally between Candidates 1, 2 and 3). Allow learners enough time to assimilate their information. If there is sufficient learner enthusiasm, this activity could be repeated with Interviewers interviewing a second or even third Candidate without any change to the 'After the interviews' activity.

As an additional activity after the interviews, the class could be divided into Interviewers and Candidates and asked to prepare the following mini-presentations:

Interviewers: who was the best candidate, and why?

Candidates: their opinions of the job, its advantages and drawbacks.

Afterwards. Exercise 1 is a letter-writing activity and Exercise 2 reviews restaurant formulae as a fill-in. Both are open-ended, but possible answers are suggested in the Key.

Unit 4 Key

PART ONE

Linking and exchanging

1
  1 C
  2 A
  3 E
  4 B
  5 D

2 A 3
   B 1
   C 4
   D 8
   E 2
   F 7
   G 6
   H 5

3 The corrected spelling mistakes are:
   Vegetable
   Tomato
   Salad
   Courses
   Grilled
   Desserts
   Apple
   Coffee

4 **Conversation one**
   1 has reserved
   2 three
   3 the table was beside the toilets

   Conversation two
   1 Because he has been kept waiting.
   2 That it is Saturday night (and the restaurant is busy).
   3 Are ... ready to order

   4 ...been waiting... half an hour.
   5 I'm sorry ...it's Saturday night
   6 ... don't you ...more staff?
   7 only just opened

   Conversation three
   1 False
   2 True
   3 True (probably)
   4 True
   5 your bill
   6 afraid we don't accept cheques

Grammar notes
   1 have
   2 will
   3 does not
   4 have
   5 has
   6 am
   7 has
   8 will not
   9 have not
   10 will

Functions/Skills notes
   1 I'd like to book a table for four, please.
   2 A 10% service charge is included.
   3 Would you like to order, madam?
   4 Do you take credit cards?
   5 I want to change my order.
   6 The smoking section, please.
   7 Could I have some mineral water, please?
   8 What would you like for starters?

PART TWO

Storyline

1 1 True
   2 True
   3 False
   4 False
   5 True
   6 True (probably)

2 1 Dollars. Pizza World's investment in Poland.
   2 The number of fast food restaurants in Poland.
   3 The number of scooters necessary for a home delivery service.
   4 The cost of the scooters.

3 1 empty
   2 competition
   3 fast food
   4 image
   5 younger
   6 delivery
   7 investment

4 1 something's
   2 've invested
   3 it's
   4 that's
   5 it'll mean
   6 won't cost
   7 'll see ... it's ...

5 1 apply   4 experience
   2 curriculum vitae 5 interview
   3 letter   6 selected

Afterwards

1 (suggested answers)
1. Following
2. pleased/happy
3. application
4. accepted
5. experience/qualifications
6. team/staff
7. salary
8. sincerely/truly

2 (suggested answers)
When for, please?
Would you prefer/like
For how many, please?
And what time?
And could you give me your name, please?

Unit 5
PART ONE

Pre-teach the vocabulary of football and sport: *fitness   to score   championship   to drop (someone from a team)   umpire*

This unit is concerned with the world of sport and, in Part Two, the ambiguous relationship between football and business.

Linking and exchanging. Exercise 1 should be done, as it provides vocabulary necessary for later. But unless your learners are interested in football, the linking of players to nationalities is optional. However, Exercises 2 and 3 provide some socio-cultural background notes to modern football.

Exercise 4. Play the cassette as often as necessary, stressing the 'business' aspect of Tommy Moore's dilemma. It is important that this is understood as it places Part Two of the unit in perspective.

Grammar Notes and Function Notes. These are optional, but the Function Notes will be useful in the role plays that follow.

Role Plays One to Three are pair activities involving professional sports people with personal problems. These situations are not designed as 'accusation vs defence' confrontations, but allow the possibility of sensitive questioning leading to an agreed solution. Try to encourage this.

PART TWO

Barnfield United is a British football team which has seen better days, a fact which Tommy Moore (its manager) does not want to admit.

Reading comprehension. Check that learners understand the storyline (i.e. that one year after hiring a new trainer, a star player and finding a new sponsor little has changed). Then get learners to read the letter from Garibaldi Valenzo. At this point you could ask what Tommy Moore should do.

Exercises 1 to 4. Play the cassette as often as necessary, making sure that by the end learners know what is at stake.

Role Play. The situation is basically simple:
- does Barnfield United keep Junio Cabral?
- what is Wim Nugteren's future?
- will Totley Holdings continue its sponsorship?
- what are the possible financial arrangements?

In the case of five participants, drop Role Four.
In the case of four participants, drop Roles Four and Five.

Afterwards. Exercise 1. Open-ended, following the decisions of the meeting.
Exercise 2. Open-ended. An essay.

Unit 5 Key
PART ONE
Linking and exchanging

1 Players try to score goals.
The referee is responsible for fair play.
Captains lead their teams during the game.
Goalkeepers try to stop goals.
Trainers are responsible for physical fitness.

Players and nationalities:
Zinedine Zidane	France	French
Ronaldo	Brazil	Brazilian
Franz Beckenbauer	Germany	German
Diego Maradona	Argentina	Argentine
Michael Owen	England	English
Paolo Maldini	Italy	Italian

2
1. increased
2. merchandising
3. survey
4. the AB class
5. breweries

3
1. Don't know
2. False
3. True
4. False
5. Don't know (or True)

4 Relegated – demoted, lowered in rank
1. disappointment
2. supporters
3. loses
4. make (meaning: earn)
5. trainer
6. abroad
7. Second Division
8. comments

Grammar notes
1. which
2. Who's
3. Which
4. who
5. Whose
6. Which
7. whose
8. Who

PART TWO
Storyline

1
1. b
2. a
3. b
4. a
5. b
6. a

2
1. Extra training sessions before each match.
2. Cut salaries by £25 if players miss training sessions.
3. No more night-clubs.

3
1. £350,000: the offer from Garibaldi Valenzo for the transfer of Junio Cabral.
2. 5: the number of goals Junio has scored this season.
3. 15%: supporters have fallen by.
4. £25: the cut in salary when a player misses a training session.

4 1 who
   2 whose
   3 who's

Afterwards

Exercise 1. Open-ended, but to reflect the decisions of the role play.

Exercise 2. Open-ended.

Unit 6

PART ONE

Pre-teach: *queue tray slot sunblinds*

This unit looks at the various problems of staff facilities in companies, and centres on vending machines.

Introduction and Listening and exchanging. Exercise 1 is optional, but could raise useful mini-discussion points about the quality of staff restaurants (useful for in-company training programmes). It is best done in pairs, with group comparison of answers.

Exercise 2. Play the cassette as often as necessary, then ask learners about the advantage/disadvantages of food vending machines in a company environment.

Exercise 3. Optional, but some of the adjectives may be useful later on in the unit.

Role Plays One to Three are pair activities. Tell learners to try to reach a compromise by using their imagination. Only if there is deadlock, give the 'Possible compromise' slips to one of the partners in each pair so that he/she can explain the compromise to the other and re-start negotiations.

Grammar Notes. These should be done as the correct use of prepositions will be necessary for the role play.

Functions/Skills notes. Optional.

PART TWO

Pre-teach: *stand-only first-aid post to predict self-service to insert to retrieve*

This part deals with a plan by a Swedish company to install food vending machines and close the canteen of Ustensilas do Brasil, a recently-acquired Brazilian company. Differing cultural assumptions are the sub-text of the conflict.

Exercise 1. This e-mail sets the scene, so the True/False questions should be done thoroughly. Check that the situation is understood by all.

Exercises 2 to 4. These deal with Antonio da Costa's presentation during an informal meeting. Play the cassette as often as necessary. The atmosphere is conflictual, and this should be pointed up.

Role Play. A group activity. The situation is basically this:
- The installation of vending machines will increase production capacity, but will not be popular with the production staff. There are also the problems of the Canteen Manager (what will happen to him/her?) and the placing of the vending machines next to the offices.

In the case of five participants, drop Role Four.
In the case of four participants, drop Roles Four and Five.

(However, in order to maintain points of argument in the role play, you should add certain of the objections of Roles Four and Five to the role cards of Three and Six.)

After the role play, give feedback about how each participant listened to the counter-arguments as well as the usual error analysis.

Afterwards. Exercise 1. An open-ended writing activity that focuses on prepositions of place.

Exercise 2. A 'vending machine' activity, this time linked to cash dispensing machines. A review of imperative verbs, followed by a possible mini-discussion for more advanced groups.

Unit 6 Key

PART ONE

Linking and exchanging

1 hot fresh menu clean bar non-smoking queue trays plates dirty noisy cold

(These are the most logical answers, but others are possible in certain places.)

2 1 b
   2 a
   3 a
   4 a
   5 b

3 1 inefficient   5 ineffective
   2 impersonal   6 impractical
   3 unpleasant   7 unsuitable
   4 unfriendly   8 inconvenient

Grammar notes

1 on (or) to
2 to (or) on
3 opposite
4 between
5 beside
6 behind

Functions/Skills notes

Open-ended.

PART TWO

Storyline

1 1 False
   2 False
   3 True
   4 False
   5 False

2 A – 250 square metres
   B over one hundred thousand dollars

3 1 beside
   2 between
   3 opposite
   4 next to
   5 near

4 a more production area
   b staff next to vending machines
   c coffee breaks shorter
   d office staff a long way from toilets
   e cost
   f staff reaction

Advantages/disadvantages – open-ended.

Afterwards

1 Open-ended.

2 insert enter press choose wait retrieve take

Unit 7

Part One

Pre-teach: *queues   check-out   promotions*

Part One of this unit deals with the differences between supermarkets and shops, and the ascension of the former to the detriment of the latter. In Part Two we examine the problems faced by a small business hoping to expand.

Linking and exchanging. Exercise 1 should be done as it emphasises the differences between supermarkets and shops as well as giving useful vocabulary.

Grammar Notes. The language of trends should be taught/reviewed here to introduce learners to the story of Mary Flanagan's shop.

Check that the reading comprehension passage is understood before continuing to Exercise 2.

Exercises 2 to 4. Play the cassette as often as necessary. Exercise 2 deals with the language of trends, Exercise 3 with general comprehension and Exercise 4 with the comprehension of numerical information.

Exercise 5. Optional.
The writing activity of James Penrose's profits is optional, but could provide a useful homework activity.

Skills Notes. Asking direct and indirect open questions.

Part Two

Pre-teach: *high-class   outlets   loan*

The story of Market Organics is typical of a small business facing a saturated market – it needs new outlets. However, many of the participants in this situation are unsure if these new outlets are either possible or desirable.

Exercise 1. A simple linking of vocabulary activity, which should be done. Check that learners understand the mechanics of supply in this context.

Exercises 2 to 4. Play the cassette as often as necessary, focusing on the conflict between Sharon Mitchell's ambitions and commercial reality. Is she being realistic? To more advanced groups, you could also point up Lenny Graft's false joviality during the radio interview.

Role Play. A group activity. The situation is basically this:
- Sharon Mitchell needs to persuade her fellow-participants that Market Organics must expand into supermarkets. But this will pose many problems (of company image, of distribution costs and of finance). Only Role Six (the Bank Manager) is in favour of a compromise, the others are for or against for different reasons.

In the case of five participants, drop Role Two.
In the case of four participants, drop Roles Two and Four.

(However, in order to maintain points of argument in the role play, you should add Role Two's objections to Role Three and Role Four's to those of Role Five.)

After the role play give feedback about the logic of each participant's arguments as well as their language errors.

Afterwards. Exercise 1. An open-ended activity based on the decisions of the meeting.

Exercise 2. For more advanced groups. An aided essay-writing activity designed to allow learners to express their own views.

Unit 7 Key

Part One

Linking and exchanging

1
1. – 3 – 4
2. – 5 – 3
3. – 1 – 5
4. – 2 – 1
5. – 4 – 2

2

	Sign	Word(s)
1	X	good
2	↗	rising
3	⋀	a peak
4	↘	to fall
5	↗	went up
6	↘	down by three thousand
7	↘	falling

3
1. There was a fire.
2. He was furious.
3. They went up.

4
1. The drop in profits in 1995.
2. The closing of the supermarket due to the fire.
3. The fall of Mary Flanagan's profits in 1997.

5 Open-ended.

6 Suggested phrases for the graph description:
'Then… they stood at about/around £8,000 until March. After that, they went up/rose/increased gradually to £10,000 by June. They fell/dropped/went down during July but rose/went up/increased steadily to over/above £10,000 in October. They fell/dropped back to about/around £8,000 in November and began to rise/increase/go up again towards the end of the year.

Skills notes

A review of direct and indirect questions.
1. how he travels to work.
2. which system they used.
3. why you left your job.
4. when the meeting starts.
5. why she wants a transfer.

Part Two

Storyline

1
founded – established
organic – naturally-produced
supplies – sells to
saturated – full
expand – enlarge

2
1. b
2. b
3. a
4. a
5. b

3
1. That's true.
2. No, I don't think so at
3. Of course not.

4
a. That Market Organics would be too expensive for supermarkets.
b. That it was too small to supply supermarkets.
c. That TV advertising would be too ambitious/costly.

Afterwards
1 Open-ended.
2 Open-ended.

Unit 8
PART ONE
Pre-teach: *tableware   to attend   reliable   fashion shows   chalet*

This unit deals with the world of department stores, and in Part Two we examine the problems faced by a supplier of a Parisian department store.

The Introduction provides general background information, but Exercises 1 and 2 of the Linking and Exchanging section should be done as they give the vocabulary necessary later on in the unit.

Exercise 3 is optional, but perhaps of interest for pre-vocational learners.

The Grammar Notes review comparative and superlative adjectives. This will be useful for the role play in Part Two.

The Functions/Skills Notes (agreeing/disagreeing) should be done in preparation for the role plays.

PART TWO
Pre-teach: *chalet   to guarantee*

Check that the roles of buyer and supplier are clarified by the reading comprehension passage.

Exercise 1. Ask learners to read the questions 1 to 5, then play the cassette once. Then ask learners to compare answers in pairs. Play the cassette a second time as reinforcement, but don't spend too long on it.

Role Plays One to Three. These are pairwork activities involving dissatisfied clients or unhappy neighbours. Although they consist mainly of statements of complaint and possible reasons and excuses, encourage learners to use their imagination to find compromise solutions.

Now we move on to the story of Bonprix and Hammat Fabrics, an Egyptian supplier of women's dresses.

Exercises 2 and 3. Play the cassette as often as necessary, doing each exercise in turn. At the end of these exercises, the relationship between Hammat Fabrics and Bonprix must be clear to all, as it is vital background to the role play that follows.

Exercise 4. Optional.

Role Play. Ask learners to read through Françoise Bernardon's 'notes' about the three potential suppliers and clear up any difficulties. The role play is a group activity. The situation is basically this:

- Recently there have been supply problems between Hammat Fabrics and Bonprix, and Françoise Bernardon is considering alternative suppliers, though she has made no final decision. But a change of supplier is always a risk, therefore the pros and cons of the situation need to be discussed with her colleagues.

In the case of five participants, drop Role Two.
In the case of four participants, drop Roles Two and Four.

(However, in order to maintain points of argument in the role play, you should add Role Two's arguments to Role Three, and Role Four's arguments to Role Six.)

After the role play, give feedback about the opinionating/agreeing/disagreeing language used as well as correcting language errors.

Afterwards. Exercise 1. A multiple-choice activity involving letter formulae and a review of comparative/superlative adjectives.

Exercise 2. An open-ended letter-writing activity.

Unit 8 Key
PART ONE
Linking and exchanging
1 fashion – (for example) Dior, Pierre Cardin, Yves Saint-Laurent, Nike
designers – people who design clothes
manufacturers – makers
up-to-date – modern
fade – lose colour
complain – state dissatisfaction
buyers – buy in bulk for companies
suppliers – sell their products to companies

2 choose – reliable suppliers
negotiate – the lowest prices
speak – good English
attend – the important fashion shows

3 Open-ended.

Grammar notes
1 biggest
2 wider
3 more profitable
4 less expensive
5 more professional

Functions/Skills notes
1 agree
2 think
3 go
4 disagree
5 think

PART TWO
Storyline
1 *1* Three weeks ago.
2 The colours have faded.
3 A receipt.
4 To replace the dress.
5 A refund.

2 *1 a* The colours fade.
b Hammat's last delivery was three weeks late.
2 That the dresses were tested for fading.
3 That there had been a strike in his country.
4 a better
b more efficient
c lower
5 That if Jakhri did not lower his prices, she would look for other suppliers.

3 Open. But possible answers: aggressive   angry   polite

4 Open-ended.

Afterwards
1 Paragraph 1: open, depending on the results of the role play.
Paragraph 2: lower – better

2 Open-ended.

Unit 9

PART ONE

Pre-teach: *drug abuse   curfew   to ban motorcycle escort*

This unit looks at a socio-medical problem common to many developed countries – the role of the small hospital.

The Introduction gives some background statistics which could raise short discussion activities. Exercises 1 to 4 are all optional, but could be usefully done as background knowledge, either as mini-presentations or as information-exchanges.

Exercises 5 and 6. Play the cassette as often as necessary. Jackie Palmer's views reflect a current social problem.

Role Plays One to Three. These are pair activities, and deal with political questions and the hypocrisy of those in power. No compromises are suggested nor possible and the aim of the role plays is to encourage questioning on the side of the journalist and imaginative evasion on the side of the politicians.

Grammar Notes and Functions/Skills Notes. These are optional, but could be useful for the role play in Part Two.

PART TWO

Pre-teach: *to clarify*

Here we focus on the problem of the hospital in Ballymullin, in Ireland. There are no easy answers to the questions raised, but compromise is possible.

Reading Comprehension. Check that the situation of Ballymullin and the implications of the population statistics table are well understood.

Exercises 1 and 2. Play the cassette as often as necessary and go over the people's petition, referring to the street demonstration.

Then ask learners to read the government's plans as well as the other facts mentioned. Point up that the time-scale is tight (close one hospital on 31 December and open the second on 1 January).

Check over the participants of the meeting – who is likely to be for or against the closure of the hospital, and for what reason?

Role Play. A group activity. The situation is basically this:
- The majority of the people of Ballymullin are against the closure of their hospital and the local economic/demographic trends seem to give them a good case. However, it is very expensive and the 'technocratically correct' solution lies with a hospital at Kilkenny. But the roles of the doctors at Ballymullin are ambiguous, they are looking after their own interests.

In the case of five participants, drop Role Five.
In the case of four participants, drop Roles Five and Six.
(However, in order to maintain points of argument in the role play, you should add Role Five's arguments to Role Three, and Role Six's arguments to Role Two.)

After the role play, give feedback on the language of conditions and cause/effect as well as correcting language errors.

Afterwards. Exercise 1. This is a fill-in exercise in the form of a letter. It reviews first conditional verbs.

Exercise 2. An open-ended interview activity.

Unit 9 Key

PART ONE

Linking and exchanging

1 general practitioner – examination – operation – anaesthetic – nurses

2 obstetrics – babies
geriatrics – old people
paediatrics – children
casualty – accidents

3 Open.

4 Information-exchange.

5 *1* longer
  2 homes
  3 closing
  4 save
  5 dangerous

6 *a* A man's retirement age.
  b A man's expectation of life.
  c The distance from a person's home to the nearest hospital.

Grammar notes

 1 it's – 'll buy
 2 take – 'll feel
 3 'll cost – want
 4 'll cook – prefer
 5 go – 'll lose

Function/Skills notes

 1 An expression of cause
 2 An expression of effect
 3 An expression of cause
 4 An expression of effect
 5 An expression of cause

PART TWO

Storyline

1 *1* False
  2 a
  3 b
  4 True
  5 a
  6 False
  7 b
  8 a
  9 False
  10 False

2 *1* 's – won't come
  2 try – 'll be

Afterwards

1 *1* persists
  2 will be
  3 will refuse
  4 is not finished
  5 will … put
  6 will … help
  7 start
  8 will stop

2 Open-ended.

Unit 10

Part One

Pre-teach: *boring   lunch break   previous engagement*

Although this unit deals with the relatively trivial subject of fireworks, it raises the wider question of business ethics in Part Two.

The Introduction is basically a historical anecdote, which may be of interest to some learners. In fact, the story of Guy Fawkes represents an interesting example of the historical banalization of a terrorist act.

Linking and Exchanging. Exercises 1 and 2 should be done, as they introduce words necessary for the role play which follows in Part Two.

Exercises 3 to 5. Play the cassette as often as necessary. Exercises 3 and 4 are for general comprehension while Exercise 5 reviews social language. With more advanced groups, you might like to ask general questions about the staff relationships at Brayton Ltd.

Role Plays One to Three are pair activities, and deal with social language – inviting/chatting/agreeing/disagreeing and making arrangements.

The Grammar Notes deal with future time and are optional, though the notes about forecasting should be checked through.

Part Two

Pre-teach: *unqualified   domestic market   to restrict   guest of honour   to be ruined   scandal   incident   to recycle   to abandon   to exaggerate*

Here we look at the problems faced by Nightspark, a manufacturer of fireworks. It is a rather unscrupulous company, and this is reflected in the attitudes of most of its managers during the role play.

Check the background information, then do Exercise 1.

Exercise 2 (also Reading Comprehension) is based on an excerpt from a newspaper. Check that learners understand the situation thoroughly, as it forms the background of the role play which follows.

Exercises 3 to 5. Play the cassette as often as necessary, homing in on Nightspark's basic dilemmas – the dangers of bad publicity and their more or less honourable stratagems to avoid it. This is more important than the forecasting language of Exercise 5 if the role play is to succeed.

Three days after the meeting. Reading Comprehension. Here we move on to the next stage, preparatory to the role play. You should ask here – What are the basic problems of Nightspark, and what should the company do?

Role Play. A group activity. The situation is basically this:
- There is a decreasing demand for fireworks in the UK due to government legislation, so Nightspark has two alternatives: either to manufacture a different product or to export its fireworks to countries where restrictions are less strict.

In the case of five participants, drop Role Four.
In the case of four participants, drop Roles Four and Six.

After the role play, give feedback on the quality of the various arguments as well as language errors.

Afterwards. Exercise 1. Open-ended, but with an emphasis on forecasting language.

Exercise 2. Social English. A letter of invitation with multiple-choice phrases.

Unit 10 Key

Part One

Linking and exchanging

1 Effigies D   Injuries A
    Fireworks C   To blow up B

2
1 anniversary   4 personalities
2 party   5 speeches
3 press

3
1 False   4 False
2 False   5 False
3 True   6 True

4
1 It was too cold.
2 There was no more ice.
3 It failed.
4 hostile – disrespectful

5
1 to see you. How are
2 Can I get you a
3 Thanks. A … please
4 there's no more … I'm afraid.
5 Let's go to the
6 Cheers!

Part Two

Storyline

1
1 Because Bratwich is an area of high unemployment.
2 Because the company has little experience of export.
3 Because of government restrictions.
4 Its sales are falling and prospects are not good.

2
1 8 (including Lottie Bruce)
2 She was the guest of honour.
3 They exploded.
4 b
5 b

3
1 Nightspark's fireworks are safe.
2 b
3 publicity
4 a
5 damages
6 False

4
1 contact Harold Brayton and try to agree on a private arrangement.
2 issue a press statement saying that Nightspark regrets the incident.
3 go and inspect the site of the explosion at Braytons.
4 go and see the injured Brayton employees to offer cash payoffs.

5
1 fairly sure   4 unlikely
2 He'll probably 5 should
3 may

Afterwards

1 Open-ended.

2
1 Corinne
2 pleased
3 well
4 let me know
5 to
6 have
7 I live
8 seeing